Action Research for Professional Selling

Action Research for Professional Selling

PETER McDONNELL AND JEAN McNIFF

GOWER

Gower Applied Business Research
Our programme provides leaders, practitioners, scholars and researchers with thought provoking, cutting edge books that combine conceptual insights, interdisciplinary rigour and practical relevance in key areas of business and management.

Published by
Gower Publishing Limited
Wey Court East
Union Road
Farnham
Surrey, GU9 7PT
England

Gower Publishing Company
110 Cherry Street
Suite 3-1
Burlington, VT 05401-3818
USA

www.gowerpublishing.com

British Library Cataloguing in Publication Data
A catalogue record for this book is available from the British Library.

Library of Congress Cataloging-in-Publication Data
McDonnell, Peter.
    Action research for professional selling / by Peter McDonnell and Jean McNiff.
        pages cm
    Includes bibliographical references and index.
    ISBN 978-1-4094-6407-5 (hardback : alk. paper) – ISBN 978-1-4094-6408-2 (ebook) – ISBN 978-1-4094-6409-9 (epub)
    1. Selling – Research. 2. Action research – Methodology. I. McNiff, Jean. II. Title.

    HF5438.2.M33 2014
    658.8'3–dc23
                                                                            2013048219
ISBN 9781409464075 (hbk)
ISBN 9781409464082 (ebk – ePDF)
ISBN 9781409464099 (ebk – ePUB)

MIX
Paper from
responsible sources
FSC   FSC® C013985
www.fsc.org

Printed in the United Kingdom by Henry Ling Limited, at the Dorset Press, Dorchester, DT1 1HD

Contents

List of Figures

About the Authors

Peter McDonnell has spent 15 years in direct sales in the financial, health and lifestyle industries. He previously spent many years as a health service manager, especially in the area of acute psychiatry. He has operated his own health care provider business, and offers consultancy advice to businesses on sales strategies and sales management. He has a master's degree in practitioner research. He works with practitioners in a range of professions, including health, business and education, and has written and presented conference papers on research-based professional development, individually and collaboratively with Jean McNiff.

Jean McNiff is well known worldwide for contributing to the lifelong professional development of practitioners and faculty in many workplace and higher and continuing education contexts. She is Professor of Educational Research at York St John University, and also holds visiting professorships at several universities internationally. She spent her early professional years in mainstream schooling and adult education before going into business for herself and then moving into higher education. She has experience of running her own business, as a shopkeeper, writer and educational consultant. Her best-selling textbooks on action research for lifelong and professional education (as sole author and collaboratively), include *Action Research: Principles and Practice* (in a 2013 third edition); *You and Your Action Research Project; Action Research for Teachers; All You Need to Know about Action Research; Writing and Doing Action Research;* and *Action Research for Professional Development.* She also writes articles for refereed journals. Jean is passionate about publishing, and developed her own publishing firm (September Books). She and Peter McDonnell formed a business partnership in 2008.

Both may be contacted through Jean's website at jeanmcniff@mac.com.

Authors' Acknowledgements

We would like to extend our heartfelt thanks to –

Margaret and Julian

Tracy and David

Henry, Joseph and Reggie, salesmen par excellence

– for all your help and support.

We also wish to thank the editorial and production staff at Gower who supported the project throughout in the most professional and kindly manner.

It has been a pleasure to work with everyone involved.

Peter McDonnell

Jean McNiff

Review of *Action Research for Professional Selling*

This is an interesting and engaging book about selling which finds the right balance between 'how to' style guidance, with research, theory and background information. The authors have created an accessible contribution to sales literature by exploring the use of reflection and other transferable skills in a sales environment, and by furthermore reiterating the place of selling skills in all of our twenty-first century lives in the ways in which humans relate to one another. The thorough investigation of action research, and the connections this has to professional knowledge, identity and self-image is both useful and fascinating, as well as helpfully backed up with case studies and examples.

*Ruth Helyer, Head of Workforce Development Team
(Research & Policy), Teesside University, UK*

This is an exhilarating book. McDonnell and McNiff give us an enlightened and enlightening perspective on action research which is thoroughly modern. The text's modernity lies in its clarity of vision and future-orientation for professional practice in higher education. Drawing deeply on inter-disciplinary theories of practice, they challenge academics in business schools and education departments alike to embrace the democratisation of knowledge for twenty-first-century learning.

*Jenny Naish, Dean of York St John Business School,
York St John University, UK*

Introduction

This book is about selling. It is also about studying and improving your practice as a salesperson. By doing this you can increase your sales, raise your professionalism and show how you hold yourself accountable for what you are doing.

This is essential in selling, because, as a profession, sales is at a critical stage. While popular books are written about selling from a 'how to do', skills-oriented perspective, little solid research is conducted into sales or suggestions made about how to improve it as a professional practice. Further, the voices of salespeople themselves are seldom heard in the scholarly literatures, nor is their opinion sought. There is an expectation that salespeople will listen to motivational gurus and management theorists and apply what they hear to their own practices. This does not honour the idea of salespeople having personalities and ideas of their own, exercising their creativity of thought and action, and developing reflective values-based approaches to their practices.

This book aims to redress the situation and show how salespeople can research their practices and offer their descriptions and explanations of practice as their personal practical theories of selling. This is essential in light of several issues.

First, while more thoughtful analysts promote the need for ongoing self-evaluation to improve practices and increase sales (for example, Tracy 1996), there is no systemic professional expectation that this will happen or should be a requirement. Therefore there is no robust practice-grounded evidence base for sales. This weakens efforts to claim sales as a profession and discipline, so it runs the risk of being incorporated into other, more legitimated practices such as marketing. The danger is intensified through the increasing centralisation of business where product and sales managers frequently assume control of all practices, including selling, through establishing direct relationships with customers (as, for example, through the advertising campaigns of Apple and Sony). Salespeople then are relegated to order taking rather than selling. Sales managers are seen as potential researchers, but sales practitioners are not. Further, while calls are made everywhere in the policy literatures for professionalism to be practice- and evidence-based, little data is available from salespeople themselves to show why this should be the case in sales. Consequently the credibility of sales as a profession suffers and salespeople remain invisible.

Second, a new customer-centred paradigm is emerging in sales as in other professions. Students' voices are heard in education and patients' rights are recognised in nursing and healthcare. While this acknowledgement may be more aspirational than real in some cases, the fact remains that new thinking about the negotiated nature of the provider–client relationship is changing professional practices, and is now entering the world of sales.

Third, business and finance, at the heart of world economies, are changing fast, under increasing pressure from intense competition for a greater number of customers who have wider choice in goods and services and ways of accessing them. What is not widely acknowledged – overlooked in fact – is that the world of business and finance is grounded in everyday selling and therefore maintained by everyday salespeople. Salespeople's work is the lifeblood of finance and the basis of the success or failure of financial economies. Yet while each salesperson has a story to tell and an explanation to give for how and why they practise as they do, their personal accounts of practice do not get into the scholarly literatures. It has to be asked why this should be the case, because salespeople speak a lot of wisdom from their practical experience. Marks and Spencer, Tesco, Walmart and other mega-retailers grew from small beginnings. Warren Buffet learned the basics of big business through selling (Schroeder 2009), as did George Soros (1998) and Richard Branson (2010). Their published stories of practice help others learn from their experiences.

You can do this too. You can offer your explanations of practice so that others may learn with you and from you. This is what this book is about. The word 'explanation' can also be called a theory. When a child learns to tie their shoelaces they have a working theory of the process. When they succeed they can explain what they did: they have generated a theory of tying shoelaces through learning from the process. The same can be said of any practice: you learn by doing and you offer an explanation (theory) by studying what you are doing. You generate a practical theory, a personal theory of practice (McNiff 2013a).

Some salespeople do this all the time. They can explain, often to considerable degrees of sophistication, what they do, why they do it, and how they learn to do it more successfully. They reflect on, re-think and re-frame their practices, and develop new imaginative ones through their learning.

These explanations do not get into the scholarly literatures. Delves Broughton (2012) says that Harvard Business School does not have sales on its curriculum; the same appears to be the case elsewhere. The dominant perception appears to be that knowledge may be found in abstract theories-in-the-literatures, even when the theories themselves are not especially relevant to the realities of emerging contexts. Sales is still often seen as a blue-collar add-on, nowhere near as respectable as, say, the silk scarves of marketing or management. Yet ironically it is also widely acknowledged that many theorists from the business world have little or no hands-on experience of direct selling, or have been a long time out of it, and, like teachers, healthcare and other professional practitioners who move into higher education and begin to teach practitioners, often lose touch with the everyday realities of what it means to be a salesperson in the real world.

Exploring why this should be the case and finding ways to challenge and transform the situation is the purpose of this book. For years we authors have talked with customers, salespersons and higher education practitioners who teach on professional education programmes in management and business. We have done this while ourselves working as salespeople involved in direct selling. At the same time we also work as academics, professional educators and organisational consultants in sales and other professional contexts, including education and healthcare. Our conversations reveal virtually universal agreement that the reason for the absence of salespeople's' voices in the scholarly literatures is because of three factors (and less acknowledgement of a fourth invisible one).

The first factor seems to be the popular image of the stereotypical hard-hitting go-getting high-pressure salesperson, as portrayed in films such as *Glengarry Glen Ross*. The image simply does not seem to go away and is possibly imprinted on the public psyche. It is often perpetuated by authors who exhort salespeople to 'Close that sale!' or 'Get the account!' – and by salespeople themselves, who often feel they have to live up to the image. We have spoken to many masters and doctoral graduates who have moved into sales, and who say that unless they are doing a hard sell, they feel they are not doing the job properly. They seem to feel pressured into abandoning the person-oriented language of reflection, relationship and consideration they learned on their work-based experience programmes and adopt instead the hype language of cutting-edge strategic innovation and ambitious competitive market edge. Although more organisations now see the benefits of soft sell, the values of reflective and collaborative practices are still not widely realised in selling practices.

The second factor is that this buying into the image by salespeople suits many intellectual and business elites, often in higher education, who still tend to see the field of research and theory as their province. There is still a widespread sense that abstract knowledge produced by expert theorists is good quality knowledge whereas knowledge generated from practitioners' experience is of inferior quality. The situation was captured by Donald Schön in the following analogy. Though now somewhat dated in relation to many other professions, it is still highly relevant to sales.

In 1983 and 1995, Schön wrote about a 'hard high ground', where intellectual elites generated 'pure knowledge and theory' (these days the high ground would also be the home of corporate elites). At the same time, there was a 'swampy lowlands', where practitioners produced 'everyday' forms of knowledge that would keep things running. The irony was, according to Schön, that the 'everyday knowledge' of the swampy lowlands was more appropriate for practical situations but was not recognised as legitimate theory, while the 'pure theory' of the high ground was much valued yet was often not particularly useful for everyday practical matters. A deeper irony was that occupiers of the high ground and the swampy lowlands all thought this was the way things should be, and no one thought to challenge the underpinning systems of power that maintained both the status quo and the system of thinking that maintained it.

The third factor is that many salespeople still see the selling–buying relationship as a competition. Customers are frequently positioned as the enemy, or as someone to be tricked or manipulated into purchasing. Salespeople new to the profession often inherit these outmoded forms of thinking from those who see themselves as 'old timers'. The image is too often communicated through popular sales books. While a new literature of sales is available, as noted earlier, this new paradigm, as with all emergent paradigms, is taking time to permeate the culture.

The fourth invisible factor is that many of us live in cultures that encourage us not to think for ourselves, and not to critique the dominant messages communicated through the culture (Alvesson 2013; Chomsky 2000; Klein 2000). We are taught through our education and political systems to be obedient to the dominant system, whatever it may be. These systems are systems of power, for they dictate who is allowed to think and speak. The point made by Schön is that people need to wake themselves up to the idea that any system that has been created can be re-created through critical engagement and thoughtful activism. Schön also made the case that the most effective way of doing this was through action research.

This idea is at the heart of this book. In recent decades a persistent revolution has been under way, where practitioners across the professions have lobbied professional power-holders to recognise them as thinkers and knowledge creators. This is happening in teaching, nursing and healthcare, the police and many other service industries. It is not yet happening to any significant extent in business education or, especially, sales education. As noted, few higher education institutions have courses on direct selling. Direct selling is not generally seen as a legitimate area of academic study let alone a discipline, nor are salespeople seen as academics, or, in many cases, capable of study. The situation is widely maintained by intellectual elites and by salespeople themselves who also do not see themselves like this (though this is probably what they have learned to think through messages in the culture).

Yet signs of hope are emerging. Some universities, mainly those positioned as 'teaching universities', are seeing the sense of developing professional education programmes for salespeople. Also, many progressive business organisations run study programmes for their personnel, sometimes supported by higher education providers who work with salespeople and sales managers. This book contributes to this work as a resource that draws on the wisdom of salespeople themselves as well as established theories in the literature. We engage with Schön's (1983) ideas about the reflective practitioner, with salespeople specifically in mind. We believe that salespeople are and must be reflective in order to keep up with the changing world of business, finance and culture. Public images need to change, but this will happen only if and when public discourses change: when the practice of selling becomes seen not as a competition with a customer but as a joint exploration of possibilities, conducted as dialogue, and salespeople are seen as reflective, competent professionals.

Further, this is now a practical necessity, for the character of consumerism is changing rapidly too. Customers are no longer passive recipients of marketised goods: in many cases they keep up with global changes faster than salespeople themselves. They educate themselves via the Internet and social media websites. They make themselves as knowledgeable about products and services as salespeople, so the nature of buying and shopping also changes (Molenaar 2013). Consequently, salespeople can often find themselves sidelined by their own customers, positioned as order-takers, or factored out of the discourse altogether.

This new consumer awareness calls for a new customer experience, which in turn requires salespeople to develop new approaches and methodologies in the buying–selling relationship. It also requires them to develop new forms of practice with customers and new attitudes towards them. Especially it calls for a new professional knowledge base that contains accounts by salespeople who show how they have researched their practices and can explain what they do, and how they hold themselves accountable for their work. This requires, as Schön said, a form of research in action on action: in other words, action research.

What's in It For You?

This book is therefore written for salespeople who wish to improve their practices, improve their professionalism and develop a dynamic research base to their work. This research base is not a traditional kind, but is one grounded in the real-life stories of sales practitioners. The book is written to support salespeople and lecturers in those workplaces, colleges and universities that now offer continuing professional development and higher degree courses in sales and selling, and to encourage other higher education institutions to develop them (see Chapter 8). By working with the book you will learn three things: (1) the most up-to-date principles and practices of successful selling and how to use them to improve every area of your selling life; (2) how to turn the story of your work into a report or dissertation through conducting your own action enquiry; and (3) how to critique dominant voices that tell you that you cannot do this; we encourage you to believe that you can.

Successful selling is based on the key principle that if you study what you are doing in order to improve it, you stand a better chance of doing it more successfully. Simply doing more of the same will get you nowhere. You need to find new ways of practising, which involves looking at what you are doing, thinking about why you are doing it and taking action to improve it in order to achieve your goals. Action research is not the usual social science kind of research where an 'expert' studies other people and produces explanations and theories about what they are doing. It is about practitioners learning on the job through researching their practice in action. Millions of people these days do action research in workplaces and organisational learning settings for which they can achieve accreditation.

The methodology of action research is similar to the methodology of sales. It involves identifying an area for investigation, understanding why this area is important, gathering data about it, taking action to improve it, showing how the situation may have improved, evaluating it, and explaining why the entire process is important for everyone in the situation. In your case, the people in the situation are you, your customer, your colleagues and your organisation. Doing action research puts you in charge of your own practice and enables you to claim that you know what you are doing, to have developed insider professional knowledge, and to have confidence that you can provide evidence to show this to be the case. Anyone can do action research; it is not difficult, but it does need a commitment to sustained learning.

Action research is a form of enquiry where you look carefully at your practice and evaluate it in a systematic way. You ask, 'What do I know about my practice? What else do I need to know? How do I find out? How do I improve what I am doing?' You gather data about your work practices and generate evidence to show what you are finding out in collaboration with other people, both peers and customers. You produce your descriptions and explanations of practice as your personal practical theory of practice, and put this into the public domain. In this way you establish the legitimacy of yourself as a practitioner (you have studied your practice), as a researcher (you can explain how you have found ways to improve it), and as a critically reflective professional (you have raised your professional status through creating an evidence base for your work and you can say why this is important). Through sharing the account of your research, whether through writing it up, putting it on social networks, producing a blog or website, or presenting it to your colleagues, you are contributing to a new knowledge base of sales research that may influence thinking in workplaces and in continuing and higher education institutions. By doing this, in collaboration with others, you promote sales as a core area of professional investigation, the same as teaching, medicine and management. You contribute to new public perceptions of sales not simply as a job done by a sharp-talker but as a reputable and highly-respected profession.

Today everyone is in sales, in some way or other (Pink 2012). University lecturers suddenly find themselves selling courses, so need to learn a whole new set of skills and knowledge. Vice chancellors, publishers and car salespeople all sell the products and services of their organisations. We need to learn and develop a new discourse to the fact that selling is no longer simply about a salesperson encouraging another to part with their money (or time, knowledge, effort or other resources). It is more about sharing these resources, or goods, so that the salesperson and customer can each enhance the quality of the other's life (Willcock 2013). While the currency of financial markets may be money, the currency of sales economies is trust and wellbeing. This book helps you learn how to combine both, and contribute to other people's and your own wellbeing.

These days it is essential for salespeople who want to develop their businesses to get professional accreditation. It is not enough simply to know what you are doing in sales. If you want to gain market edge you also need to be able to say how you have come to know it, why you need to know it, why this knowledge is important, and how it may be used. Being able to say why you are doing something moves everyday selling practice into research practice: you move from simple descriptions (what you do) to explanations (why you do it) and analyses (you can say why this is important and why others should listen to you).

The book is written for salespeople in any context, whether you are selling ships, houses, cars or ideas. It is an important book because the demographics of selling practices are changing too. More people are setting up their own businesses, and Internet access and globalising practices are expanding the field by the minute. Selling can often be lonely, given that most salespeople work on an independent basis, whether for a company or themselves; it is a competitive area where only those who are good at their jobs will survive. It is essential therefore that you should develop your understanding of what you are doing, and be able to explain this. The book will help you by explaining how to research your practice in action.

It does this by focusing seriously on selling as a field of research. Most books on sales tell you how to increase sales by developing your skills. Not many books tell you why you should study your practice or how you can get accreditation for doing so, and how putting your own theories of selling into the literatures can position you as an expert knower of your practice from whom others can learn. We hope we have done this here, and we wish you good luck with your studies and continuing success in your selling.

To Note

All the case study material in this book is drawn from the real-life accounts of salespeople, with their permission, and with our thanks. Some names are genuine, others not, again with permission. All have been glad to contribute in what has turned out to be a collaborative effort.

Thank you, too, for reading the book. We hope you will enjoy it and find it useful for your work. We would be glad of any feedback that would help strengthen the ideas and writing, so please connect, and perhaps also if you would like to make your story public through future publications. This would further contribute to developing a view of selling as collaborative enquiry. If you write to us we will respond, perhaps not immediately, but we will.

You can reach Peter McDonnell at mcdonnell.peter@outlook.com.

You can reach Jean McNiff at jeanmcniff@mac.com and you can read more of her books and resources at www.jeanmcniff.com.

PART I
Sales and Action Research

Most salespeople want to find ways of increasing sales. This means studying and evaluating what you are doing, identifying those aspects that are working well, and taking action to improve any that need attention.

For many salespeople, selling is not simply about making money. It is also about promoting a product they are committed to, possibly that they have designed or produced. Selling their product gives meaning to a salesperson's life: they contribute to other people's wellbeing, and thereby to their own. All parties potentially benefit, learn and grow through the interaction.

Increasing sales and contributing to mutual wellbeing means checking what you know and need to know, and possibly need to improve about both sales and your practice. These issues are the focus of Part I, which consists of three chapters.

Chapter 1 is about sales. It outlines some common understandings of what sales is and some debates in the field. It helps you take stock of what you know and what you need to know, and where you locate yourself in the debates.

Chapter 2 is about action research. It outlines common understandings of what action research is, and some of the debates in the field. It explains how to research your practice in order to increase your sales and give deeper meaning to your life. It also helps you appreciate how you are contributing to knowledge of the field of sales.

Chapter 3 is about why you should do action research. It explains how doing something well involves studying and evaluating practice, which is core to extended professionalism. Continuing professional development becomes a normal part of practice. By saying that your practice is research-based, you contribute to your own professionalisation and to the professionalisation of sales.

Chapter 1

What is Sales? Becoming a Reflective Salesperson

This chapter deals with the critical issues raised in the Introduction, as follows:

- The changing nature of sales and the need for a new focus that shows the collaborative nature of relationships between salespeople, customers and business colleagues. This is contrary to many current sales practices that still position customers as competitors rather than as partners. Practitioners' knowledge can contribute to this new focus.

- The need for sales to be seen as a credible area for study, and for research to be conducted by salespeople themselves, as well as by business leaders and academics in higher education. Salespeople's experiential knowledge should be seen as the grounds for valid theories, and their practices as a form of theorising in action.

- The need for critique. The fact that salespeople's knowledge is not highly valued stems mainly from a lack of critique about what counts as legitimate sales research and theory, who is qualified to do research, and how theory and practice may be linked. This situation needs interrogating.

Engaging with these issues has implications for you as a salesperson. If you wish to have your knowledge and yourself valued, you need to make sure you are up to date with current thinking in the field. You also need to develop the capacity for critique so you can show that you do not simply take things for granted but engage critically. You need to turn yourself into a discerning reflective practitioner and theorist.

The chapter contains advice about what you need to know in order to do this:

- What you need to know about sales.

- What you need to know about the methodologies of selling.

- What you need to know about researching sales.

What You Need to Know about Sales

As noted in the Introduction, higher education institutions do not often take sales seriously as a topic of study or include it on their curricula. To study sales in higher education you would need to register for, say, an MBA or similar, where you would study topics such as the theory of business, marketing, economics and strategic management. The expectation would be that you would apply the theory to your practice. Currently research into sales usually appears as part of sales management research (Guenzi and Geiger 2011). This involves learning how to manage a sales workforce, delegate responsibility and forecast trends.

This model of applying theory to practice has until recently been dominant across all disciplines, including teaching, nursing and healthcare, the military and police, and other public services. However, in recent decades it has come in for severe critique on the grounds that it still keeps theory and practice apart as separate realms of study and separate fields of discourse, so there is little connect between abstract theory and real-life social wellbeing. It is also recognised that linking theory and practice means including the voices of practitioners themselves, otherwise it becomes an artificial exercise, like reading about yoga but not doing it. Now, therefore, most higher education institutions have begun to incorporate practice-based forms of research onto their curricula, many in the form of action research (see below). However, this is still not happening to any great extent in business or sales, although awareness is growing in some places. You can contribute to changing this situation, and turn sales into a serious topic of study, but this means first appreciating what is involved. A key element is learning to become critical (Carr and Kemmis 1986). Critique does not mean finding fault with something, but interrogating what is going on in order to understand it better and improve it. It also means critiquing our own situatedness: we interrogate what is going on *for* us as well as *around* us. Primarily it means checking whether we are thinking what we have been taught to think, or are questioning and thinking for ourselves.

Here, then, we

- consider what we need to know about the nature of sales;

- think critically about how current practices and understandings have been influenced by historical, social and cultural developments;

- consider some implications for how the purposes of sales may be understood.

WHAT DO WE KNOW ABOUT SALES? WHAT ARE OUR CURRENT PERCEPTIONS?

Sales is generally understood as the interactive process between a salesperson (you) and a potential customer, which leads the customer to make the decision to buy the product. The outcome is that both lives may be enhanced. The customer gets the product they want (a new helicopter, a course that helps them improve their skills), as well as the joy and personal enhancement the experience of buying can bring (Appadurai 1988; Baudrillard 2005), and you and your company continue to thrive.

As a salesperson you are in a dual position spanning your customer's and your company's interests. You are able to influence the quality of your customers' lives, as well as your own, through providing them with a service or product they want. You are also able to influence what happens in your product company. Behind the shop windows on the high street are the thousands of people who actually make up the company. You are the main communication channel, the interface between them and their customers. You are the only person in the entire system with a working knowledge of the product and the customer's needs. This means you have considerable responsibility, opportunity and power for influencing the success of your company, as well as your own. In the 1970s and 1980s television comedy *Open All Hours*, the shopkeeper Arkwright would go out of his shop at the end of each day and look back at the front window, to take stock of what it would look like from a customer's point of view and see what he needed to do to enhance their experience. You do this too. You reflect the customer's perspective back to the company. This is central to ensuring the quality of a good customer experience as the basis of a successful sale. Watkinson (2013) comments:

> ... if you focus on delighting your customers ... profit becomes a well earned by-product of a business that is successful in a much broader sense.

> *You get the pleasure of knowing that you are making a positive*
> *contribution to people's lives, and customers [will] reward you with*
> *their loyalty and do your marketing for you (Watkinson 2013: 5).*

HOW HAVE WE COME TO KNOW WHAT WE KNOW ABOUT SALES?

Social movements do not just happen, but are subject to all kinds of influences. Current perceptions of what sales is and what it is for have been greatly influenced by historical, social and cultural developments. Here are some of the most important aspects.

Historical influences

It is widely accepted that sales should be seen as a fundamental aspect of human endeavour. Perhaps all economic evolution is premised on the fact that someone somewhere (an individual person or a government) sold an idea or a product (a toothbrush or a means of communication) to someone (a customer), who then bought or bought into the product or the idea. This may also be seen as the basis of social marketing (for example, Lee and Kotler 2011), the idea that marketing principles may be used for social and environmental benefit. Appadurai (1988) explains how, although commodities may be seen as objects of economic value, they also become symbolic of personal and social value. Bourdieu (1992) develops these ideas in discussions of symbolic power: if you have something other people desire they see you as having social capital and this gives you symbolic power, usually over them. In many contexts people don't buy unless something is sold; and, because a lot of selling is done subtly, people often don't realise they have been sold to. This is the basis of the concept of product placement: in the James Bond films, for example, branded articles such as champagne and cars are placed prominently.

Throughout the history of direct selling the principles of the sales process have remained constant, although the objects of exchange and forms of currency may have changed (in most places money has replaced physical goods, and credit cards have replaced cash). These principles are evident in the earliest records, including those of the Phoenicians or Indo-Romans who travelled the silk and incense trade routes and the merchants who travelled extensively to sell their goods. There was also a long tradition of 'the peddler' who both made and sold their wares direct to customers, often at street markets as well as through door-to-door selling. The traditions remain today, especially in the more indigenous forms of trade found in traditional Traveller communities in Ireland and in North African souqs and bazaars. Over time indigenous goods have been supplemented by new ones: Raleigh for example is reputed to have brought tobacco to the UK from the Americas. Nor was it always necessary to move far away from home to conduct one's business. For example, prostitution, probably the most ancient profession, used the principles of pre-call planning and preparation, prospecting, presenting selling points and closing the sale (Gilfoyle 1994). Evidence remains in the preserved city of Pompeii in the form of paintings on the walls of a brothel, noted for its frequently long queues of tourists.

Trade also contributed to the development of empires and colonies through the activities of merchant adventurers visiting other countries to look for articles to trade. A striking example is the story of how Hong Kong was taken from China by the British in 1842 as a punishment for China's temerity in opposing Britain's selling opium into China, turning many people into addicts (Hoe and Roebuck 1999).

The Industrial Revolution

In the eighteenth century the onset of the Industrial Revolution in Europe began to influence the nature and purposes of selling. Now goods were mass-produced through the development of sophisticated machines, and concurrent economic expansionism enabled customers to acquire goods that were not essential to basic living. As manufacturing developed, manufacturers moved further and further away from customers by hiring representatives to market and sell their products for them. Selling became more remote and compartmentalised, which led perhaps inevitably to a separation of activities such as designing, managing, marketing and selling into different categories according to a factory model of production.

A great leap forward in the development of sales in the 1870s came in the form of Richard W. Sears, a railway employee in the US, who developed the idea of the sales catalogue which could be distributed by rail; this brought about an explosion of sales among a far-flung populace by creating a desire and the practical means of realising it. Prairie farmers in Kansas were able to order goods including pianos and even houses from the catalogue of the company that later became Sears Roebuck.

The rise of Fordism and Taylorism

In the nineteenth and early twentieth centuries two related trends became prominent: Fordism and the theories of Frederick Winslow Taylor. Henry Ford initiated standardised piecework, where people worked on an assembly line using specialised tools for a particular job. These practices were strengthened by Taylor's theory of scientific management, which aimed to improve efficiency and productivity through the organisation of work as units that could be measured in minutes and seconds. These practices have had long-lasting influence, giving rise to a culture of efficiency and rationality, premised on assumptions that the methods of scientific management may be transferred to all practices. In Chapter 2 we discuss ideas about the kind of knowledge and thinking that underpin these practices, especially in relation to how technical rationality has until recently been the dominant philosophy of business, management and commerce.

This philosophy of technical rationality can be seen everywhere. It has led to the mass marketisation of knowledge as a product to be sold, exported and imported (see Callahan's 1964 classic *The Cult of Efficiency* for how these views have influenced education; Ball 2007, 2012 gives contemporary analyses). It is also visible in the prolific advertising of professional education courses, especially those that promise to turn practitioners into experts in ten easy steps. This view is contrary to that of the craftsperson (Sennett 2008), who spends long years of training and journeying to learn the core knowledge and skills of their craft. While philosophers such as Marcuse (1964) pointed out the potential dangers in practices that separated people from the goods they created, the practices continue today. An over-emphasis on scientific management ignores the idea that people can give meaning to their lives through their relationships with one another. It also ignores the potential technologisation of human endeavour, especially when consumerism becomes a means of social control (Aldridge 2003) and the resultant dangers of alienation where people feel separate from others and their own practices.

Alienation has indeed become a common experience of social living today and has significant implications for how salespeople understand their practices. Do they see their products simply as objects to be sold, rather than the realisation of their own beliefs and social commitments? In Miller's (1994) *Death of a Salesman*, Willy Loman becomes disenchanted with life and work because it has little meaning for him. How do salespersons see customers? As sources of income rather than as people in themselves, means rather than ends? Scientific management legitimated a brash style and aggressive form of selling: while some people saw its usefulness in producing quick results and fast money without the expense of ethical considerations, by the 1970s and 1980s it was generally being recognised that a short-term 'get-rich-quick' philosophy was damaging to personal and organisational integrity. A need began to be expressed for new approaches to sales.

Social and cultural influences

People are more aware now of what they wish to buy because of the influence of social and cultural changes, as follows.

The education of consumers through the information revolution

The age of the Industrial Revolution has transformed into the information age through virtually universal access to computers and the Internet, so consumers are aware of purchasing choices. Armchair shopping is easy and rapid feedback on products and services is at our fingertips: ease has become as important a criterion as quality. A negative comment online can prejudice the sale of a product; and the buying behaviour of consumers is changing (see Molenaar 2013 about 'the new shopping').

The networked society through social networking

The networked society forecast by Castells in 1996 is now a reality through the Internet, smart phones and social networking. People take control of their lives, as shown in social movements such as Occupy and the Arab Spring. The election of Barack Obama was coordinated largely through mobile phones. A downside of this is that change, once started, can be difficult to manage, with unpredictable outcomes.

Educational curricula

Schools teach students to use digital technology and make choices, and students' interactions in turn influence institutional practices (as in student satisfaction surveys). Students have become customers. Further and higher education link knowledge with business (McNay 1995; Olssen and Peters 2005) and run courses in entrepreneurialism. Many higher education institutions have themselves become businesses and strive for market lead (many, however, adopting outmoded forms of selling, which is where education can learn from sales – see Chapter 8).

The social nature of information

Information is often acquired socially (Brown and Duguid 2000); you can learn as much from talking with a colleague over the photocopying machine as from a book. Information is shared, developed and transformed. Knowledge about practices (what Gibbons et al. 1994, call Mode 2 knowledge) becomes as valuable as knowledge about abstract theories (Mode 1 knowledge).

Movement in the workforce
Ease of travel and the relaxation of immigration laws have led to economic and political formations such as the European Union, so migration of the workforce is commonplace. This has sometimes led to demographic change and imbalances of employment within the indigenous population (Inglis 2008). It is often cheaper to locate business offshore or recruit overseas labour than to recruit from the national workforce.

Political and financial influences
Perhaps the greatest impetus for increased consumer awareness has been the crisis in banking and commerce, where bankers and industrial elites have moved business away from shareholders' interests to their own. Pre-arranged bonuses for bankers have often had disastrous economic fallout for customers (Cooper 2009). Financial corruption, linked with political corruption (O'Toole 2009; Ross 2009) has given rise to a new managerial class fuelled by short-term targets and rewards, ignoring the fact that customers and shareholders will lose in the process (see Martin's 2011 analyses of how this happens). Many salespeople have contributed to this corruption, selling, for example, unsustainable mortgages.

SOME CONSEQUENCES OF THESE CHANGES FOR SALES PRACTICES

All these developments towards the 'new consumerism' (Bauman 2005) carry significant consequences for how sales may be understood. This is especially so in relation to a new kind of alienation, a 'culture of emptiness' (Alvesson 2013), where easy access to goods can lead to a culture of immediate gratification and short-termism. The acquisition of goods becomes seen as more important than learning to do something well. Instant quick-fix knowledge is prioritised over lasting wisdom. It values the acquisition of factual and procedural knowledge, 'ownership' of facts and skills, rather than the wisdom that guides how to use them. Further, says Alvesson, and others such as Klein (2000), most of the reasons for the alienation are deliberately hidden from our conscious awareness through the use of propaganda systems and media control (see below).

This culture of emptiness is explored by Putnam in *Bowling Alone* (2000). He explains how people's social capital (connectivity with family, friends and work colleagues) is eroded through changes in work, business and family structures. Putnam writes about America but the same kinds of fallout are visible in most countries.

Similarly, Sennett (1998) explains how many people lose their way through new cultures of entrepreneurialism and flexible working. For him it becomes 'the erosion of character', where 'character' refers to 'the ethical value we place on our own desires and on our relations to others' (p. 10). He asks:

> How do we decide what is of lasting value in ourselves in a society which is impatient, which focuses on the immediate moment? How can long-term goals be pursued in an economy devoted to the short term? How can mutual loyalties and commitments be sustained in institutions which are constantly breaking apart or continually being redesigned? These are the questions about character posed by the new, flexible capitalism (Sennett 1998: 10).

A culture of having rather than being

Many people judge their worth in terms of what they have, rather than what they do: the standard of excellence shifts from scoring a goal in a local football league to purchasing a mobile telephone. Consumerism becomes a virtue, to be taught and encouraged through educational curricula (Ball 2007). Institutions that aim for market lead are considered virtuous while advice from local communities is considered interference (see Teixeira and Dill 2011). Fromm's *To Have or to Be* (1979) provides a key conceptual framework. A 'having' view leads to identifying ourselves by our possessions, so friends and family become things we have, not people with whom we are in intimate relation: see also the popular *Affluenza* (James 2007), where 'having more' leads to 'wanting more', yet ultimately leaves the acquirer unfulfilled.

Being a visitor or a participant in community

Bodies of literature to do with communities of inquiry and practice (Garrison 2011; Wenger 1999) explain how people come together to share ideas and develop practices; but unity is destroyed when some people see themselves as visitors rather than participants. They drop by rather than engage, a hurried view of practice that has no time to put down roots but moves on for fear of missing out ('fomo' according to the Urban Dictionary).[1]

---

1   See http://www.urbandictionary.com/define.php?term=fomo.

Control of the public mind and the urgent need for greater critique

Most importantly: authors such as Chomsky and Barsamian (2001) and Foucault (1977) explain how people are persuaded to obey dominant messages that permeate the culture through strategies such as predatory advertising (see Packard's 1967 *The Hidden Persuaders*). Further, they are persuaded to believe that obedience is their idea in the first place through what Foucault (1980) calls 'regimes of power' and 'governmentality', where systems are put in place to control people's thinking. Chomsky and Barsamian (2001) explain how easy it is to use intimidation and violence to control how people think in totalitarian societies; in democratic societies, however, more subtle means such as mind control are used. We are persuaded to see ourselves as free to choose between products, but fail to realise that we are not free to decide whether to opt for a 'having' culture in the first place. We are persuaded to be content to vote for the winner of the X-Factor rather than actively engage with our communities. Even then we do not see that we buy into a subtly imposed system; we do not see the system, let alone challenge it, perhaps yet another example of bread and circuses for the masses.

This brings us to what we believe are some of the uses and purposes of sales.

What Do We Know about the Uses and Purposes of Sales?

These ideas about the dangers of alienation and the need for community have become visible in newer critically-oriented sales literatures, with an increased focus on the development of personal relationships and the values base of selling. Popular books speak about values-based selling (Bachrach 1996), trust-based selling (Green, 2006), customer-centred selling (Jolles 2000), customer-centred strategy (Jenkins 1997), and customer-experience management (Schmitt 2003). However, with some notable exceptions (for example, Tovey 2012, Johnstone and Marshall 2013 and Watkinson 2013), key points are still missing, including:

- The customer is still positioned as the 'other', a means to the salesperson's ends. There is little mention of the need for selling to be seen as contributing to personal and social wellbeing.

- The books continue to focus on the skills and competences of practice, but not about the need for developing a research base to practice.

The move is notable also in the wider business literatures: for example Carroll (2012) and Willcock (2013), who emphasise the need for collaborative practices in business. However, they still miss the central point, that the voices of practitioners are absent. Texts still work from the assumption that the author produces the theory and practitioners apply it to their practices. New perspectives need to be developed that see:

- The need for dialogical approaches in sales: customers and salespeople find ways to contribute to personal and social wellbeing through engaging with the other in mutually reciprocal practices. Until this happens, the traditional view of 'them and us' will continue.

- The need for practice to be seen as the grounds for research and to make clear the processes involved in theorising practices. Until this happens, sales will continue to be a poor relation to marketing, advertising and strategic management, all of which have their own research bases, and these disciplines will continue to be seen as separate categories of practice. Sales itself needs to become a distinctive area of study that is related to and possibly incorporates those other areas, and build a strong knowledge base to show the processes involved. This is what we try to do in this book.

Appreciating what this involves means looking at the sales process itself, and developing new perspectives that see the methodologies of sales as a legitimate form of process research that can generate a strong theoretical base to inform new practices and new thinking.

What You Need to Know about the Methodologies of Selling

In this section we look at what is involved in the sales process, and organise it initially as two processes:

1.   the principles of selling;

2.   the procedures and action steps of selling.

THE PRINCIPLES OF SELLING: THE CONCEPT OF AIDA

Most people working in the field agree that sales is a systematic process involving certain activities based on certain principles. The principles state that in order to sell someone something you have first to attract their *attention* and capture their *interest*; this then gives you the opportunity to arouse their *desire*, which will lead to their taking *action*. This concept, originally developed in marketing, is commonly known as AIDA and is well known in sales. It is a commonsense process that you can see played out in virtually any social interchange. Whatever you are doing in a sales process falls somewhere under the umbrella of AIDA.

Here are two real-life examples of AIDA in action.

1.   You are walking down a street and suddenly a man outside a restaurant throws a plate on the ground. He has your attention: you think, 'What on earth is he doing?' He then begins talking to you engagingly, inviting you into the restaurant, promising two meals for the price of one; he now has your interest. You go to the door of the restaurant and see the lovely candles inside, smell the wonderful aromas of the food, and are greeted warmly by a manager. Your desire for food and a great experience are aroused. You move into action and walk through the door.

2.   Think of the late great Steve Jobs when he introduced a new Apple product. First there was a lavish advertising campaign and a spectacular set – this got your attention. The lights lowered and the auditorium hushed as people's interest was aroused. Steve Jobs walked on to the stage carrying the latest Apple device with arm outstretched, leading to a unanimous groan of desire from the crowd. At the end of the presentation, people could not wait for the stores to open so they could take action and purchase the product.

You can see the same process at work everywhere: for example, when you try to teach a new subject matter to students or launch an advertising campaign for human aid. It is an everyday process of communication and interaction. Even dogs do it when they want you to take them for a walk and bark at the door or bring their leads to you. This concept of AIDA – Attention, Interest, Desire, Action – can be further refined. Some authors add 'E' for 'Evaluation', some 'S' for satisfaction, and some 'C' for confidence; but 'AIDA' stands for the basic process. We all do it without analysing it or calling it anything: we learn how to do it from birth (see Pink 2012). You would think of the concept of AIDA at every point in the sales process, when you are prospecting, appointing, presenting and consolidating (see below).

Now let's move the thinking into research, which means knowing and showing the difference between describing and explaining. If you were to tell someone about what you did, as in the example above, you would describe your actions to them (say *what* you did). If, however, you wanted to tell them why you did it, or evaluate its effectiveness, you would give them explanations (say *why* you did it). You would turn your descriptive account into an explanatory account. You would say something like this:

> *A new restaurant had opened just down the road and represented some competition for us. The restaurant was placed so that customers saw their restaurant before they saw ours, as we are tucked away around a corner. Each day I could see customers going in there – quite a few; I actually counted them – so I decided to find a way of getting them to come to our restaurant first rather than the new one. I bought some cheap plates at the surplus store, stood on the corner outside our restaurant where everyone could see me, and smashed the plates on the ground when I saw people coming. Many were curious and came up to see what I was doing. When they came near I welcomed them and gave them a leaflet offering two meals for one, and showed them the restaurant. The manager was waiting at the top of our small flight of steps. He smiled and came down the steps to greet them and escort them into the restaurant. Once they set foot on the steps they were with us.*

You would probably reflect on what you had done and whether it had been effective. You could say:

> *I think it was a useful strategy because it did get people's attention and brought them into the restaurant, so I will continue doing it for the next week or so. However, I cannot sustain it because the interest value will probably wear off in time and it may also be difficult in the winter months. My colleagues and I will need to find other strategies: perhaps advertising in a targeted way or try circulating leaflets with special offers. We will need to assess then how we are getting on. Watch this space.*

Look at what you have done here. You have reflected carefully on your practice and begun to evaluate it. You have considered different courses of action and given reasons. You intend to take collaborative action with your colleagues to find new and better ways of doing things.

Look at the strategies employed. You have done the following:

- identified an issue you wanted to investigate (the threat of new competition down the road and possible loss of customers);

- explained why it was an issue (loss of customers meant less business);

- produced data to show what was happening (made notes about how many customers were going into the other restaurant);

- decided on a possible solution (bought the plates);

- taken action (stood outside the restaurant and smashed the plates on the ground);

- continued to look for data to show what happened (customers showed interest and came up to you);

- evaluated the success of your action (customers came into the restaurant);

- continued to smash plates outside the restaurant because the strategy was successful, but are now considering new ways of working.

In other words, you have researched the event in action and come up with a possible solution. The plate-smashing strategy may not have worked, so you could have tried something else, monitored progress and adapted that as a main strategy instead.

This process of investigating something in action, reflecting and evaluating the process and its outcomes, and finding new ways of doing things with others is called action research – research in action for action. Like AIDA, it is a commonsense process, much of which we all do intuitively. You try out different strategies that help you succeed in what you are doing. You reflect on what you are doing, consider what worked well and what could have been done differently, and decide on a new course of action. You take action and say why you are taking this course and not another, and how it may be more effective. You can analyse and explain what you do as follows:

- explain what you are doing and why you are doing it;

- gather data to show the situation as it is and as it continues to change;

- explain why you are gathering a particular kind of data rather than another;

- explain why you are taking a particular action rather than another and what you hope to achieve;

- assess the success of the action in relation to what your data and evidence show you;

- explain why the action you have taken is important;

- explain how you are going to change your thinking and practices in light of your evaluation.

When you tell people what you are doing you give them descriptions of actions; when you do research you give them explanations for actions. Doing research is always about explaining what you are doing; doing action research is about explaining and analysing how you are finding how to do things better, and producing evidence to show that this is the case. The point of this book is to help you make explicit what you are doing, and to develop conscious awareness of it so you can explain to others why you are doing what you are doing.

THE PROCEDURES AND ACTION STEPS OF SELLING

Now let's look at what procedures and action steps are involved in selling. These are commonly agreed as:

- prospecting (including planning);

- connecting and appointing (including contacting and identifying needs);

- presenting (including closing);

- developing (including consolidating and asking for referrals).

Each step involves specific actions, as follows:

Prospecting

This involves:

- Searching for new clients: Who is going to buy from you? Where will you find them?

- Targeting specific clients: Who do you know? How will you make contact?

- Qualifying them: Deciding whether or not they are able and likely to buy from you.

- Planning: Planning how and when to approach them, and what to do so you will not be rejected.

Connecting and appointing

This involves:

- Establishing your own credibility and that of your product and company.

- Explaining the distinctive benefits of your product and company.

- Communicating why people should believe that you will do as you say.

- Deciding how you respond to the universal question, 'What's in it for me?'

Presenting

This involves:

- Establishing trust as the basis for a sustainable relationship.

- Identifying your customer's needs and helping them to articulate them; matching products to needs; presenting your product as a potential solution to identified needs.

- Creating a desire for your product.

- Pointing out the benefits of your product (and yourself) over others: establishing your value through communicating your values.

- Citing other people who have purchased your product and the benefits they gained.

- Negotiating objections: explaining how a customer's concerns will be dealt with and resolved satisfactorily.

- Agreeing a price.

- Closing the deal: the customer agrees to purchase the product.

Consolidating and developing

This involves:

- Ensuring that orders are in place and delivery dates arranged.

- Checking that all questions have been asked, all information given.

- Ensuring customer aftercare: immediate follow-up to check all is well; asking your customer to reiterate the benefits of your product.

- Looking for possibilities to develop more business together.

- Asking for referrals to recruit further customers.

The question now becomes, how do you research your sales practice in action? How do you come to the point where you say you know something now that you did not know before? Here is a brief overview of what is involved: this is developed in Chapter 2.

What You Need to Know about Researching Sales in Action

Action research is a commonsense approach to help you find ways to develop your sales practice, and to study and record what you are doing as part of your continuing professional development. You ask, 'What am I doing? How am I doing it? Why am I doing it? How do I check whether I am doing it well? How can I do it better? How can I contribute to the professionalisation of myself and others, and to raising the status of the profession?' By asking these kinds of questions you can systematically investigate what you are doing, and produce your own descriptions and explanations (that is, theories) of selling. Doing this enables you to show how you have evaluated what you are doing and found ways of doing it better.

As noted, this approach is so grounded in commonsense that, when people begin doing action research, they often say, 'This is what I am doing in any case, as part of my everyday practice. How is action research different?' How it is different is that you identify something about your work that you wish to investigate further, monitor what you are doing and gather data about what you are doing as you go. You use this data to generate evidence to show how things are improving (or not), and this evidence comes to act as the basis for your claim that you know what you are doing and can justify what you are saying. You need to test the validity (truthfulness) of this claim by inviting other knowledgeable people to look at your findings and say whether or not they believe you, that is, whether you are justified in claiming that you have improved your practices or understand better what you are doing: in your case, this could be whether you have developed good practices, increased sales and built up a portfolio of returning customers.

This idea about a claim to knowledge, or a knowledge claim, is important because, by researching your practice in action you are moving beyond only professional development, and moving into knowledge creation and theory generation. You are showing how you are moving beyond knowing the tricks of the trade; you know the trade itself. You are moving beyond knowledge of skills and moving into knowledge of practice.

However, issues and questions arise, especially in relation to who is qualified to do research in sales and generate valid theories, and who says so. Here is a snapshot of what is currently going on in the field of sales research.

A BRIEF OVERVIEW OF SALES RESEARCH

We said at the beginning of this chapter that, until recently, sales was not seen as a particularly credible topic of research. Buehrer, Simon and Bieraugel (2013) state that out of 779 articles in the *Sales and Sales Management Magazine*, 701 (90 per cent) were about sales management, not about the practices of sales.[2] A common assumption is that the job of salespeople is simply to sell. They become good at their jobs by applying established theories of selling but not necessarily by questioning those established theories, or coming up with new ones. It is assumed that they will acquire new knowledge of sales though attending sales training courses or through learning from more experienced salespeople in the field and speaking the script they are given.

This view has been a dominant assumption in most higher education settings too. Universities have run courses for sales managers whose job is to manage the salesforce (Moran and Brightman 2001), and less so for on-the-job salespeople. In effect, universities and sales managers have tended to reflect the same attitudes towards salespeople as the attitudes that traditionalist salespeople have shown towards customers – that they are non-thinking consumers. It is assumed that some people are positioned as authorised knowers (Apple 2000) and others who are assumed not to know.

The analogy by Donald Schön about the high and low ground of professional practices (page 4) is perhaps symptomatic of this view. When this analogy is used in a sales context it becomes clear that such hierarchical forms are themselves inappropriate, because salespeople, like their customers, are also discerning consumers. Salespersons themselves wish to be recognised as thinking persons and have their practical experiential knowledge valued and recognised as legitimate. This is what this book aims to do.

Overcoming these dilemmas can mean tensions for salespeople and academics alike. For salespeople, it means accepting the responsibility of researching their practices and explaining what they are doing and why they are doing it, that is, theorising their practices. This means developing more analytical perspectives to explain what they know and how they come to know it. They become active knowledge creators. Salespeople re-identify themselves as 'thinkers and knowers', not only 'doers and appliers'. By evaluating and revising their understandings of practice they develop expert knowledge. This can be discomfiting, because developing new self-perceptions involves moving out of comfortable habits of mind and developing possibly risky ways of thinking. It means not rejecting established theories in the literatures so much as incorporating them into personal processes of learning and developing new forms of knowledge.

---

2   See   http://www.ncsmweb.com/images/proceedings/pdfs/Competitive/6_-_Buehrer_Simon_and_ Bieraugel_3-page_abstract_pp17-20.pdf.

Academics often experience similar tensions of identity too. Acknowledging salespersons as legitimate knowledge creators means giving up position power as legitimised theorists. This can be difficult for some academics as being called a theorist brings symbolic capital and power, though others gladly join the move towards egalitarianism.

Self-critique becomes essential, because it means recognising that practice begins in the mind: how we think influences what we do. Changing our practices means changing our thinking. Changing the hierarchical nature of institutions and systems means changing the hierarchical nature of how we think. Dominant forms of thinking draw on linear metaphors that take the form of a → b → c → n. People are seen as located in separate roles and compartments (such as sales, marketing and advertising): these are usually hierarchically ordered and power constituted. We need to think instead in terms of webs of connected relationships (Figure 1.1) where the relationships themselves become as important as the objects they connect. This becomes a mutually reciprocal system, whose flow is inspired by values and facilitated through dialogue. We need a new dialogical paradigm of sales.

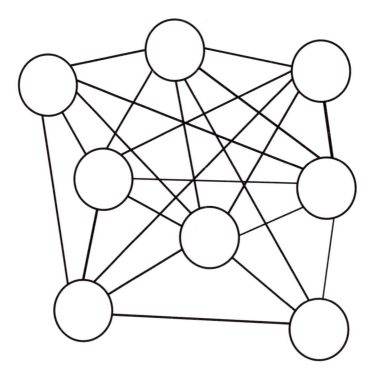

Figure 1.1   Web of interconnected relationships

We also need to appreciate that we are born into a specific culture and learn to think according to cultural norms. Bourdieu (1990) speaks of the *habitus*, which contains its own systems of thinking, as well as systems that say what is right and proper to think. 'How we think' is also termed 'logic': each habitus has its own accepted form of logic. In industrialised and knowledge-creating societies the dominant form of logic is linear and fragmented, and also causal: we think 'If I do this, that will happen', or 'If I do this, they will do that.' This is the theoretical basis of most social science, including management, leadership and education. Management tends to be seen as organising someone; educating is seen as educating someone; sales is seen as selling to someone. The assumption is that the 'other' is a foreign country, closed off by its own boundaries. Many of us live our lives in mental straitjackets, not appreciating that we have the option of not thinking in this way.

We authors take the view, along with many contemporary philosophers (for example, Macmurray 1961; Macdonald 1995) and management and organisational theorists (for example, Senge 1990; Wheatley 1992) that people are in close relationship with one another. What one person does influences another: we are in relationships of influence. Each person lives by their own values, which need to be negotiated through dialogue.

These ideas are central to new approaches to sales and business. We need to see individuals and groups of people as in a symbiotic relationship, where what happens to one influences the other. We need also to develop new forms of logic to help us describe and explain what we are doing as salespeople. Our customers are not our rivals, or dummies to be duped into buying. They are people in their own right, with whom we are in a social and spiritual relationship. The theoretical base of sales needs to move from seeing customers, colleagues and competitors as 'them over there' to 'us working together to achieve an improved quality of living for everyone involved'. And there are pragmatic reasons for this, too, because people's perceptions and tolerance of sales change as they acquire more information about products, prices and availability.

These ideas are developed throughout the book.

Summary

This chapter has explored ideas about what sales involves. It makes the point that practitioners need to adopt a critical perspective towards how practices and perceptions are influenced by historical and socio-cultural factors.

They also need to interrogate their own positioning in sales situations to be clear about how they understand the nature, origins and purposes of their work in sales. This can most effectively be achieved by researching the field in action, that is, undertaking action research into sales. This becomes the focus of Chapter 2.

Chapter 2

What is Action Research?

In Chapter 1 we introduced the idea of action research. In this chapter we consider what action research is, how to do it and what its benefits may be. We consider how it is different from other kinds of research and how you can choose different methodologies for different purposes. This requires you to know some of the underpinning assumptions of action research, and research in general, and how these assumptions inform conceptual frameworks and related ideas.

The chapter is organised into the following sections:

- What do I need to know about action research?

- What are some of the underpinning assumptions of action research?

- What are the main theoretical and conceptual frameworks of action research?

This leads to Chapter 3, which is about why you should do action research and how it will help you as a salesperson.

What Do I Need to Know about Action Research?

This section deals with the following:

- What is action research?

- Who can do action research?

- How do you do action research?

- Where did action research come from?

WHAT IS ACTION RESEARCH?

Action research is a practical way of looking at your work to check that it is as you would like it to be. If you feel that it is already good quality, you describe and explain to others what you are doing and why you think they should agree with your explanations. If you feel that your work could be better, you find ways to improve it. You check with others to get their feedback on what you are doing, and you use this feedback to help you evaluate your practice and your thinking.

Because action research is done by practitioners, it is sometimes called by other names, including practitioner research, practice-based research and action-oriented research; and because it involves you thinking about and reflecting on your work, it also becomes a kind of self-reflective practice. You use the learning arising from your reflection to inform new practices; and this in turn generates new action and reflection. Consequently, the methodology of action research is understood as cyclical and transformational (see Figure 2.1 on page 45).

Action research is used around the world in a range of contexts and is perhaps most widely used on professional development courses across the professions. However, professional development is no longer seen simply as about improving skills and competencies but more as a matter of in-depth professional learning for personal, social and organisational improvement. This is where action research often becomes a methodology of choice, because it emphasises that practitioners themselves need to accept the responsibility of studying and evaluating what they are doing, and show how their work may contribute to their own and others' benefit. Consequently action research is seen as a powerful means for generating evidence-based practice. You show through the dissemination of your research that you have achieved a high level of practice knowledge that encompasses skills, competencies and underpinning philosophy, so people can feel confident about your knowledge and professionalism. Given that it is now commonplace for practitioners to achieve accreditation for their studies, including masters and doctoral degrees, action research has gained increasing credibility as a form of transformational learning that can influence processes of personal, social and organisational change. Action research is now used also for inter-professional learning (for example, Littlechild and Smith 2013), where practitioners work and learn with and from one another in collaborative communities of enquiry. The profession of sales has much to contribute to these inter-professional debates by showing how dialogical and collaborative learning can influence others' learning and practices.

To appreciate fully the scope of action research it is important to appreciate what doing research means, what makes action research distinctive and especially how it differs from everyday practice.

Doing research

There is a considerable difference between taking action and doing research. The core difference is that action refers to what you do; research refers to how you find out about what you do.

When you want to find out about something, you research it. This may lead you to do an informal or formal research project. At the beginning of your research project you ask a question such as, 'How do I do this? How do I learn this?' This becomes your research question. At the end of the project you say, 'I know how to do this. I have learnt it': you claim that you know something now that you did not know before. Your knowledge may take several forms: you may have discovered something that other people already know (how a car engine works), and you may have created knowledge that is new for you (how to change a tyre, or understand better the relationship between people's motivation and their productivity). In academic language, saying you know something is called 'a claim to knowledge' or 'a knowledge claim'. The aim of all research is to enable a researcher to make a knowledge claim, which means you can describe and explain what you did in order to come to the point that you now know it. This involves gathering data and generating evidence to test the validity (truthfulness) of your provisional knowledge claims against other people's critical feedback.

There are many different ways of doing research, and each one tends to be used for a particular purpose. You would use scientific forms of research to study science and technology; and interpretive research to understand more about how people work and act. You use action research to study what you are doing in order to understand it better and improve it.

As well as different kinds of research, there are also different ways of doing action research, ranging from what Reason and Bradbury (2008) and Torbert (2001) call 'first-person action research' to 'third-person action research'. First-person action research is when you study yourself and your practice: you ask, 'How do I increase my sales?' Second-person action research is when you help other people, perhaps in a consultancy role: you ask, 'What do they need to do to increase their sales?' Third-person action research is where you hope your research will have wider social impact: you ask, 'Will this particular strategy or product help a developing country to become more self-sufficient?' There is no 'correct' way, except what is right for the circumstances at the time; all perspectives can be valuable, according to different circumstances. It is up to you to choose your approach and positionality. 'Positionality' and 'positioning' refer to how you position yourself and others in the research, and you need to be able to explain why you have made your choices.

An especially helpful typology of researcher positionality in action research is by Herr and Anderson (2005: 31). They outline a continuum of positionalities, from insider to outsider, as follows:

- insider researcher studies own self/practice;

- insider in collaboration with other insiders;

- insider(s) in collaboration with outsider(s);

- reciprocal collaboration (insider–outsider teams);

- outsider(s) in collaboration with insider(s);

- outsider(s) study insider(s).

In this book we tend to speak from a first-person perspective (though we are aware that other people may not share this approach), because we believe that, whatever perspective you adopt, you need to make appropriate decisions about your own courses of action. We also believe that practitioners should study their own practices before they can advise other people about what they should do.

DIFFERENT CONTEXTS FOR ACTION RESEARCH

Go to http://jeanmcniff.com where you will see many examples of practitioners celebrating their work and sharing ideas. Examples are available of how people have studied their practices and gained higher degree accreditation for doing so: see the 'Theses' section. There are also stories of how people living and working in difficult circumstances such as township schools have presented their work at international conferences and have been recognised as powerful theorists. A free booklet is available on action research (at the 'Booklet' tab), which you can download and use for your own purposes.

What action research is not

To appreciate what action research is, it may be useful to consider what it is not. It is not traditional social science research, which is the dominant form of research in the practices and literatures of sales management, business, marketing and other related areas (for example, Guenzi and Geiger 2011). Traditionalist social science research (referred to from here on simply as 'social science research') has several clear characteristics:

- Social science research tends to be done from an externalist perspective, where a researcher observes, describes and explains other people's actions and behaviours. Social scientists ask, 'What are those people over there doing? How do I describe and explain their actions?' They generate theories by studying the behaviours of other people, disseminate those theories, and assume that other practitioners will apply them to their own practices. Common theories used by sales practitioners include the concept of AIDA and buyer-oriented theories; and there are hundreds of theories related to management and organisational issues. Action research, on the other hand, assumes that practitioners can generate their own theories of practice by studying their practices. They draw on established theories in the literature and decide whether to incorporate them into their own practices.

- Social science research aims to demonstrate a cause and effect relationship between variables: for example, smiling more often engenders a more positive response in people (Kim and Yoon 2012). The premise is that 'if I do x, y will happen', on the basis that it is possible to predict and control what will happen in the future. Traditional research in sales uses social science methods extensively, for example, to make forecasts about sales figures and recommend appropriate practices. Sajtos (2011) gives a comprehensive overview of sales forecasting techniques, pointing out, however, that there is seldom a correlation between forecast and outcome, given the complexities of organisations and market forces. He also cites Armstrong's (2001) description of the sales forecasting process, which closely resembles the action research process outlined in this book, as follows:
  - formulate problem;
  - obtain information;
  - select methods;
  - implement methods;

- evaluate methods;
- use forecasts

(Armstrong 2001: cited in Sajtos 2011: 180).

A key criterion for judging the quality of social science research is therefore its capacity for replicability (when the same observation or experiment can be done again by someone else in the same conditions with the same results) and generalisability (when the results can be generalised to all like circumstances). Social science research is the main kind of research currently used in sales management.

Action research does not set out to explain what other people are doing from an externalist perspective, or to demonstrate a cause and effect relationship. It is usually conducted from an internalist perspective, where practitioners investigate and evaluate what they are doing in order to develop and improve it. They can do this individually or collectively. They ask:

• What am I doing?/What are we doing?

• Am I doing it well?/Are we doing it well?

• Do I/we need to improve anything?

• If so, how do I/we improve it?

• Why should I/we?'

Action research does not take a hypothetical stance, but is located in the real world and starts from where you are. It is often associated with lifelong and work-based learning across the professions (Kemmis 1982; Zuber-Skerritt 1993).[1] Practitioners place the interests of the service user at the heart of their work and ask, 'How do I/we help you?' By helping other people, practitioners by default help themselves.

WHO CAN DO ACTION RESEARCH?

A special attraction of action research is that everyone can do it. So-called 'ordinary' practitioners such as salespeople can do it as much as people who

---

1   See also helpful guides at http://www.open.ac.uk/cobe/docs/AR-Guide-final.pdf and http://www.jeanmcniff.com/ar-booklet.asp.

are assigned 'official' responsibility, such as sales or business managers and academic directors. You do not need any specialised knowledge, although you do need to learn an appropriate academic language and concepts if you wish to get accreditation for your studies. This idea of everyone being able to do action research is a particularly distinctive and attractive feature. It challenges assumptions that research is a specialised practice. This is not the case. You actually begin doing research as soon as you ask, 'How do I do this?', and then follow this up by explaining your reasons for wanting to do it, trying something out and gathering data about what you are doing.

Some people see action research as a form of problem solving, but this is not quite accurate. Imagine, for example, that you are learning how to ride a bike. You get on, you fall off. You get on again, and fall off again. You think, 'I am not getting this. What should I do differently?' and you decide that perhaps you should get up some momentum to stay upright. You do so, and it works, so you can say that you have started learning how to ride a bike. This process so far is action learning, that is, learning in and from action; it is problem solving but it is not research. Research takes things further. Research happens when you identify something you need to find out about, imagine a way forward, try it out, gather data and generate evidence, see if it works (evaluate it), and change practice in light of the evaluation. You also test the validity of emergent knowledge claims and make your research public. This also enables you to explain the significance of what you are doing and what you now know. You can repeat this process indefinitely as your understanding and expertise in the area grow. As soon as we find an answer to something, a new question tends to emerge.

Action research therefore is more than problem solving though it can start with problem solving. It is always about offering descriptions and explanations for what you are doing (this is a key characteristic of all research, including action research). To claim that a process is a research process you must show how it involves explanations. In academic language, an explanation (which also contains a description) is often called a theory (see Chapter 1). When you offer descriptions and explanations of what you are doing you can say you have generated a personal theory of practice, that is, you can describe and explain what you are doing.

HOW DO YOU DO ACTION RESEARCH?

Doing any kind of research, including action research, is a systematic process. It is not necessarily a linear process which looks like a → b → c → n. Research means showing a process that is related and coherent, not haphazard, rather like the Greek story of Theseus who went searching through the maze for the Minotaur. The goddess Ariadne gave him a golden thread to tie to the entrance so he could retrace his footsteps. It is like this when you do research: you begin at the beginning and you arrive at a point where you say you know something that you did not know before (you make a knowledge claim). You can trace your steps back and forth through the process. Although you may have taken a circuitous pathway you can show and explain the process you have gone through. This does not necessarily mean that you come to an 'end point', because new questions emerge.

All forms of research share common features. These are:

- identify a research issue;

- identify research aims;

- draw up a research design and plan;

- gather data;

- establish criteria and standards of judgement;

- generate evidence from the data;

- make a claim to knowledge;

- submit the claim to critique, that is, test its validity;

- explain the significance of the work;

- disseminate the findings;

- link new knowledge with existing knowledge
(McNiff and Whitehead 2011: 26).

Action research follows this same process except that it invites the researcher (or group of researchers) to ask critical questions about the job in hand, as follows:

- What do I want to investigate?

- Why do I want to investigate it?

- How do I show what is happening at the moment that leads me to want to investigate it?

- What can I do about it? What will I do?

- How will I show how things develop as I take action and the situation improves (or not)?

- How will I check that any conclusions I come to are reasonably fair and accurate?

- How do I change my practices in light of my evaluation?

- How do I explain the significance of what I am doing?

You can bring this schema to virtually any situation in sales (as in Chapters 4–7 of this book): for example the kind of questions you would ask may include:

- *What do I want to investigate?* I need to improve my conversational skills. I never seem able to find the right words when I am with customers, such as when I am presenting. How do I learn to do this?

- *Why do I want to investigate it?* It is important to improve my conversational skills because I am probably losing customers. Many don't see what I am getting at. They don't seem to relate to me and switch off. I am not realising my aims and values of successful business practices.

- *How do I show what is happening at the moment that leads me to want to investigate it?* I can produce data that show I am not achieving as high sales figures as others on my team, so I do need to do something about the situation. To get some ideas about what I need to do I need to gather some data to see myself in action.

- *What can I do about it? What will I do?* I could ask a colleague to come with me on my next appointment and observe me in action. She can give me feedback. I will also ask her to do some role play with me when we are off duty; or I could sign up for one of the courses that the company runs. I will read some books and articles about how to improve my listening, conversational and communication skills.

- *How will I show how things develop as I take action and the situation improves (or doesn't)?* I will continue to gather data about how I am improving my conversational skills. I can videotape myself in action during the role play or on the course and keep records of how I am learning new skills, such as listening more rather than speaking impulsively. If I use these skills in my business meetings I can probably gather data to show how my improving skills are helping to increase my sales figures; I will keep records over a period of three months to see if this happens.

- *How will I check that any conclusions I come to are reasonably fair and accurate?* If I feel I am improving my conversational skills I will ask colleagues to observe me when I practise role play during our free time. I will also ask my colleague or manager to accompany me on sales visits and observe me in action, if possible over a period of three or four visits. After every sales visit I will ask the customer if they feel I have listened to them appropriately and taken their views properly into consideration, and I will keep a record of their responses.

- *How do I change my practices in light of my evaluation?* I will continue practising and refining my conversational skills. I will continue to read and work with others. I could even volunteer to be a coach for other colleagues who may feel I can help, having learned through studying my own experience.

- *How do I explain the significance of what I am doing?* Good listening and communication skills are at the heart of building the kind of trusting relationships that are core to successful selling. I shall continue to develop my own capacities, and urge other colleagues to do the same.

This process appears repeatedly throughout this book. We also introduce the idea that you can ask different kinds of questions at different points of the process, and we develop this point in appropriate chapters.

Many practitioners like to know where action research came from and how it relates to other disciplines. Here is some general information.

WHERE DID ACTION RESEARCH COME FROM?

Most writers say that action research began in the 1930s, in the US, with the work of John Collier, acting as commissioner for Indian affairs, and with Kurt Lewin, a German refugee who fled from the Nazi regime, and now worked as a social psychologist in industrial settings (Noffke 1997). Lewin believed that workers would be more productive if they felt actively involved in decision making about their work (Lewin 1946). His ideas have remained influential, especially his idea that studying practices could be conceptualised as a cycle of steps: observe–reflect–act–evaluate–modify. One cycle could turn into another cycle – see Figure 2.1.

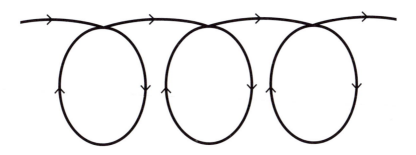

Figure 2.1   Ongoing cycles of action reflection

Other sourcebooks give examples of action research in different contexts and disciplines: for example, Greenwood and Levin (2007) speak about the industrial democracy movement in Norway. In the 1950s action research was developed vigorously in education in the USA, and linked strongly with the free schools and progressive education movements of the time (Miller 2002), as well as with democratic labour movements (Zinn 2005). An influential theorist was John Dewey, who wrote about education and democracy (1916) and the need to learn from experience (1963). However, action research began to go into decline in the US in the late 1950s with the launch of the Russian Sputnik and the decision to divert funding from educational/social work into scientific research in support of the space race.

In the 1960s and 1970s action research was taken up in the UK, especially with the work of Lawrence Stenhouse (1975), who was working with teachers in curriculum development and initiated the 'teacher as researcher' movement. He recommended that teachers should research their practices in classrooms and produce evidence to show how they were improving them. This work was later developed by John Elliott through the Ford Teaching Project that promoted the idea of teachers as researchers (Elliott 2007). The idea took hold in other professions, such as nursing and social services (for example, Rolfe 1996, 1998). Since then, the idea of people investigating their own practices has developed across the professions and is seen today as a major form of professional education, though not yet in sales. If you can produce your account of your action enquiry as a salesperson, you would be pioneering the field.

What Are Some of the Underpinning Assumptions of Action Research?

We said above that 'positionality' and 'positioning' is a major theme in action research, especially whether you adopt an outsider stance, where you do research on others, or an insider stance, where you do research from inside a group, or from somewhere between, or a mix-and-match. You can also do a self-study form of action research, where you study yourself and your own practices and relationships while you are inside the group. Virtually everything is permissible provided you give reasons for adopting your chosen stance.

Your decision depends on a range of factors, including your own commitments, especially:

- your ontological commitments;

- your epistemological commitments;

- your methodological commitments;

- your social and political commitments.

YOUR ONTOLOGICAL COMMITMENTS

Ontology is the study of being, and is strongly linked with values: you can say, 'I believe in freedom' or 'I value independent thinking', in which case 'freedom' and 'independent thinking' become values and guiding principles. Our ontologies influence the way we see other people. In sales you relate to your customer in terms of how you position them: do you position them as an object and a means to an end (yours) or as ends in themselves? These ideas are developed further in Chapter 6.

A core aim of action research is to try to realise your values in practice, or at least to live in the direction of your values. If you value independent thinking, you try to ensure that you encourage others to think independently. Do you as a salesperson encourage customers to make choices that are right for them? Ensuring a good customer experience probably depends on whether you as seller interrogate what you are doing in relation to their and your own needs. This is a far cry from forms of predatory sales where a salesperson aims to hoodwink customers into a quick sale.

Sometimes we do not manage to realise our values, which can act as a warning sign for possible action. Not doing so can lead to emotional and cognitive dissonance (Festinger 1957); for many people, trying to resolve the dissonance becomes the beginning of an action research project. Sometimes personal values can conflict with organisational values, often leading to considerable dilemmas but providing fertile ground for an action enquiry.

Things can get tricky when you work with people who do not share your values. How do you negotiate values? How do you justify your personal values stance? These matters are pivotal if you are, for example, selling in a country with different cultural values from your own. How do you negotiate your working relationships? How do you judge the quality of what you are doing? How do you cope when selling to customers, or working for a company, who may have different aims and values from you? There is no standard answer to such dilemmas except to adopt a critical stance and think through your ontological and moral commitments, which include trying to appreciate the other's position from their own perspective. This is where a body of literature about the experiences of salespeople could help other salespeople to learn and develop appropriate strategies for action.

VALUES IN CONFLICT

Savinda and Eric work for an independent company which charges a fee to carry out simple walk-in health checks for the public. Savinda's profit margin figures are consistently lower than Eric's, but her overall turnover is higher because she is popular and people ask for her. Eric sees fewer people but persuades most of them to buy the health supplements and alternative remedies the company stocks. They regularly have good-natured debates about this. Savinda says her first responsibility is to her customer, and will not sell something just to make more money when they already pay for a service. Eric counters that this is

> incorrect and unfair to the company that pays them. They should be loyal and maximise profit. Eric says he is more of an asset to the company because of his higher profitability. Savinda points out that a much higher percentage of her customers return for follow-up, so she is more effective in the long run.

YOUR EPISTEMOLOGICAL COMMITMENTS

Epistemology is to do with the study of knowledge: you study what you know and how you come to know it and use this knowledge for personal and social enhancement. There are different kinds of knowledge, but sometimes people see one kind as more important than others. Which kind of knowledge you aim to generate influences the kind of research you undertake. Here are some ideas about the relevance of different kinds of knowledge for sales.

Different kinds of knowledge

It is popularly understood that there are three main kinds of knowledge: 'know that', 'know how' and 'personal knowledge'.

- 'Know that' refers to knowledge of facts and figures. It is the kind of knowledge referred to in most textbooks on sales, sales management, marketing and organisational development. You would read, for example, 'The figures show that sales are rising' or 'We are increasing profit margins'. You would produce empirical data to back up your statements of fact. 'Know that' usually takes the form of statements of fact, often called 'propositional knowledge'.

- 'Know how' refers to knowledge of skills and procedures, so is often called 'procedural knowledge'. This kind of knowledge is also found in most textbooks on sales and associated disciplines: for example, 'I know how to present and sell my product' or 'I know how to maintain good records'. You would demonstrate your skills to back up such statements by, say, showing a video of yourself demonstrating how to maintain a sales log.

- 'Personal knowledge' refers to experiential or tacit or embodied knowledge, and the wisdom you acquire through experience. Personal knowledge enables you to be sensitive to your customer's needs or the atmosphere. You know when the time is right to ask for the order or whether to leave it until later. If people asked you how you did it, you would probably say, 'I have learned through personal experience.' Polanyi (1967) says we know more than we can say: as a salesperson you rely on your intuitions, such as when to suggest moving on in the sales process. Sennett (2008) says that a professional who is expert at their craft (their capacity to make and do things in the world) balances their tacit and explicit knowledge:

In the higher stages of skill, there is a constant interplay between tacit knowledge and self-conscious awareness, the tacit knowledge serving as an anchor, the explicit awareness serving as critique and corrective. Craft quality emerges from this higher stage, in judgments made on tacit habits and suppositions (p. 50).

All these kinds of knowledge are related. We present them separately for analysis, but in real life you would use them all. No one kind of knowledge is 'better' or 'worse' than any other; they are different and appropriate for different situations. When you do research you need to know the differences so you can explain what you are doing and why you are doing it.

Changes in priorities of forms of knowledge

Until the 1950s, the idea of 'know that' and 'know how' was dominant throughout all fields of enquiry, including sales, though the situation has changed in recent years. Earlier sales literatures had a strong focus on factual and procedural knowledge. If you followed received wisdom you would aim only to close deals (Girard 1989; Hopkins 1982). This was also the basis, as noted earlier, of the main academic literatures: you should apply abstract theory to your practice for successful outcomes.

Attitudes and practices have changed. It is now acknowledged that knowledge is uncertain; you do not know what the next moment will bring. Popper (2002) said that you cannot predict what will happen because you cannot predict what you will know until you know it; Berlin (1990) challenged assumptions that (1) there was an answer to everything; (2) the answer could be found; (3) once the answer was known, everyone would agree with it. This is simply not the case. Take for example the reality that Jews and Muslims both claim Jerusalem as their capital. These issues are about conflicting rights, not about right and wrong. In sales you do not know what is right for your customer, and often they don't know what is right for themselves. A sales business meeting needs to be a joint exploration between you and your customer where you are both finding out about the other and how to make the situation beneficial for all.

Further, knowledge itself is often socially constructed. Brown and Duguid (2000) explain how people learn by talking through dilemmas; and Senge (1990) sees social interaction as the key methodology for organisational learning and change. For you it means acknowledging your customer as an astute person who often knows what they want, how they can get it and why they want it. It is your job to match your product or service to their perceived needs and wants, and explain why they should choose your product rather than someone else's and why they should trust you.

Knowledge is seldom static, because it is always the property of a live knower. Therefore it is important to maintain an attitude of enquiry in everything, to ensure, as Feynman says (1999) that your knowledge is for tomorrow, not yesterday. He also speaks about 'standing on the shoulders of giants' (a metaphor commonly attributed to Isaac Newton), coming to know new things from existing bodies of knowledge. This is not to say that systems of ideas are necessarily displaced, as Kuhn (1996) maintains: many knowledge systems rub along happily together, as when, for example, Muslim, Hindu and Christian places of worship exist side by side on the same street. The task is to know what you don't know and what you need to find out.

YOUR METHODOLOGICAL COMMITMENTS

Methodology is about how things are done at a procedural level in terms of the reasons and purposes of the research. The methodological assumptions underpinning traditional social science methodologies and those of action research are different.

In traditional social science research methodologies, it is assumed that research will provide a final answer, and that the answer will be found through demonstrating a cause and effect relationship between variables: that is, you say, 'If I do this, that will happen.' In action research you do not aim for a final answer so much as new questions. You begin from where you are, and move forward through a process of enquiry. You ask, 'I wonder what would happen if … ?' and try out your different options, testing and evaluating them as you go.

The methodology of action research is therefore always open and developmental, and is frequently untidy, haphazard and experimental. Mellor (1998) and Law (2004) both speak about the 'messiness' of the methodology.

Winter (1998) speaks about 'improvisatory self-realisation in action research' and Dadds and Hart (2001) speak about 'methodological inventiveness', where we try different ways of working until we find the one that is right for the time and place. You do this in sales: you try out different strategies until you find the one that is right for you and your customer. Hawken (2010) observes:

> Whenever one is faced with two different paths, each with its certainties and unknowns, the cardinal rule in strategic planning is to take a path that allows you to shift to the other path if your initial decision should prove wrong. As futurist Peter Schwartz advises in his book The Art of the Long View, choose the option that gives you the most options in the future (Hawken 2010: 157).

Action research can provide a rigorous methodological framework for systematically investigating and trying to improve practices in the light of not knowing.

There are political implications in these views. A traditional social science epistemology and pedagogy holds that knowledge is created by an expert who passes it to a passive recipient; this is also a basic assumption of most professional education processes and mainstream schooling (see Chomsky's 2000 view of formal education as a process of 'mis-education'). Action research assumes that all practitioners are agents, regardless of whether they work in universities, shops or factories: we create our knowledge, frequently collaboratively, and use it according to our own values orientations, as follows.

YOUR SOCIAL AND POLITICAL COMMITMENTS

A core premise of action research is social intent. It is a methodology of change, and the change is always assumed as towards the social good. For example, in the mid-twentieth century, Paulo Freire (1996) and Orlando Fals Borda (1982; Fals Borda and Rahman 1991) encouraged citizens to mobilise and challenge the colonisation of their land by landowners. Freire saw knowledge sharing as a means for doing so. This was the basis for Participatory Action Research, a form of action research that focuses on reclaiming property rights and goods. This tradition is actively pursued by action researchers such as Stringer (2007).

Social intent is significant for you, because you may sometimes have to decide whether to sell a product to a customer or not. While selling itself is ethically neutral, you are not, so you need to think responsibly about what you are selling. Think of a situation where you may question the use of the product, which perhaps you know will serve the interests of manufacturers or providers rather than customers. Yet the sale may be massively profitable: you may be forfeiting a healthy profit if you don't sell. Think of the recent debacles when US mortgage lenders deliberately agreed to investment packages that led to the destruction of banks and the global economic crash: there are massive profits to be made from such dealing (see Martin 2001 for some excellent analyses). Soros (1998) says that financial values should not be the most important ones to live by: this kind of focus, he says,

> ... is justified when the objective is to determine the market price, but it ignores a wide range of individual and social values that do not find expression in market behavior. They ought not to be ignored in deciding issues other than the market price. How society should be organized; how people ought to live their lives – these questions ought not to be answered on the basis of market values (Soros 1998: 43).

You always need to balance customers' interests with your own, and make appropriate choices.

What Are the Main Theoretical and Conceptual Frameworks of Action Research?

Now let's consider the main theoretical and conceptual frameworks of action research. This kind of strong theoretical base, linked with the literatures, is essential if you are on a degree programme.

The most important theoretical and conceptual frameworks of action research are to do with the nature, conditions for and uses of emancipatory change. This reflects a founding principle, articulated originally by Marx (online 2013) that it is not enough only to interpret the world: the aim is to change it. This was a driver for the 1930s and 1940s critical theory movement that provided much of the impetus for action research (see Chapter 3). While the critical theorists' aim was to understand the historical, political, economic, cultural and social factors that led to current circumstances, and make suggestions about how these could be changed, they did not move specifically into change theories. Action research was one of the methodologies that took up the challenge of implementing processes of change and studying their effects.

This part covers the following:

- the nature of change;

- the conditions of change;

- the uses of change.

THE NATURE OF CHANGE

Action research accepts that change is not a single event but an ongoing process of transformation (Schön 1973); this process mirrors the natural world order. Theorists working from this perspective (for example, McNiff 2013a) draw on philosophical traditions such as chaos and complexity theory that emphasise processes of immanence (Spinoza 1996) and emergence (Capra 1996; Johnson 2001).

These ideas, and action research itself, are also used extensively in management and organisational research and theory. Early theorists who laid the foundations of dynamic theories of organisational change include the following:

- **Ludwig von Bertalanffy**, a biologist whose ideas about the processes of interrelated living systems led to his developing open systems theory, later developed as a general system theory, emphasising the need for organic systemic thinking.

- **Urie Bronfenbrenner** who developed the idea of ecological systems theory. This sees human development as an ecological system, where all parts of the system are interlinked.

- **Russell Akoff** who was involved in developing operations research, systems thinking and management science. He has been influential in encouraging interactive and participative approaches in management.

- **Peter Checkland,** an action researcher who developed what he calls 'soft systems methodology', a commitment to seeing all parts of a social situation as interrelated and mutually influencing.

- **Peter Churchman** who developed critical systemic thinking, emphasising the moral dimensions of work and organisational life (adapted from Flood 1999).

Later theorists of organisational change include Morgan (2006), who proposes metaphors of organisation: for example, organisations as machines, as organisms, as flux and transformation, and others. Theories of organisation reflect the underpinning epistemologies of their creators. Some think in static fragmented ways (Frederick the Great wanted his soldiers to be mechanical men), while others think in dynamic ways that reflect the transformational nature of organic systems and ever renewing processes of growth (Kauffman 1995). Mitroff and Linstone (1995) show how organisational growth can be encouraged through unbounded forms of thinking. These dynamic forms emphasise the interrelationships between the development of theory, behaviour in organisations and management practice (Mullins 2013: 42). The principles of complexity theory (Capra 1996; Johnson 2001; and others) include the transformational nature of organic systems and ever renewing processes of growth and the relatedness of systems and processes (Kauffman 1995). Nonaka and Takeuchi (1995), Henderson (1996) and Wheatley (1992) apply these forms of thinking to organisational growth through collaborative learning.

Some authors (for example, Pearson 2011) incorporate these ideas into action research. McNiff (2013a) links generative transformational processes with ethics: growth itself is ethical, reflecting the ethical natural order. Growth is always towards openness and ongoing transformation. When a growth process becomes distorted and inward-looking it self-destructs. It is when power-hungry people try to interfere with the natural order and close down open processes towards freedom that unethical practices intrude and growth is inhibited.

THE CONDITIONS OF CHANGE

While 'change' may be an abstract concept, change processes are not. Marr (2012) says there are no abstract forces in history (p. xv): history is made by the everyday interactions of everyday people. Some people have greater social and political influence than others, and use their influence to encourage or inhibit processes of change. Some actively try to inhibit change when it threatens their own positioning.

Social change cannot become social transformation without the political will of individuals and collectives. People themselves need to decide how they wish to live and which practices and relationships will enable them to get to where they want to be. Their choice of relationships with self, others and the wider social and natural environment are informed by their ontological, epistemological, methodological and political commitments. Look at how this plays out through different contexts of relationships and its relevance for your sales practices.

Relationships with self

Think about how you see yourself. What is your self-image? Do you see yourself as competent and capable? Do you look after yourself properly? Do you write your own script, or speak someone else's? It is widely understood that healthy social relationships begin with healthy care for the self (Foucault 1997; Rand 1964). Senge et al. (2005) speak of the importance of being present and self-aware in each moment. Populist self-help books such as Cranfield (2007) speak about personal balance, while Langer (2010) and Dweck (2012) explain how to reverse the damage of self-distorting perceptions. This has implications for you, whether you are attending to your spiritual wellbeing and achieving a right work–life balance. If not, you cannot serve your customers or company well. 'Working to live or living to work' still holds true. A useful strategy for learning personal harmony is what Hermans and Gieser (2012) call 'dialogical self-theory', where you conduct an internal dialogue to help you make implicit understandings explicit and available to your conscious mind for inspection and analysis, to decide how to change your self-perceptions and attitudes.

Relationships with others

The idea of dialogue is essential for developing appropriate social relationships too. Key theorists Buber (1937) and Bohm (1996) believe that dialogue refers not only to the words people speak but also to an openness of mind, an always-already attitude towards the other and a readiness to listen, understand and learn. Often, so-called dialogue takes the form of two monologues, when people talk past each other: while Person B is speaking, Person A is thinking of the answer they will give. They respond to what they think they hear rather than what is actually said. Buber says that this willingness to listen depends on how we position the other, whether we develop an 'I–It' or an 'I–Thou' relationship. Some people see others as 'Its', that is, objects and means to further their own ends. Others see other people as 'Thous', that is, ends in themselves with whom one is in relation.

Dominant forms of sales theory continue to adopt an 'It' perspective to customers. While they may speak about 'customer-centred relations' and 'ensuring good customer relationships', the assumption is still that customers are 'them' with whom 'we' need to interact; undertones of power never go away; the sub-text is always how to persuade the Other to part with their money.

Each salesperson has to decide their own positioning in relation to customers, and the purpose of their work; these matters cannot be mandated. Do we agree with Macmurray (1957), who sees self as an agent in the world who is working with other selves as agents? How do we position our customers? Are they equals in dialogue? How do we manage relationships with customers who adopt a power-constituted stance themselves and position us as non-equals? How to develop dialogically-constituted relationships? There are no quick-fix answers to these dilemmas, but at least you can make a start by interrogating your own self-perceptions and honestly evaluating how you perceive your relationships with customers.

Relationships with the wider social and natural environment

There is increasing awareness of the interconnectedness of people at local and global levels and to seeing the world from the other's perspective for developing intercultural knowledge and skills. This is especially important in domestic and international contexts of doing business in cultures not one's own.

The literatures regarding cosmopolitanism and locals are helpful here (see also McNiff 2013b). Hannerz (1990) for example explains how 'locals' have a stay-at-home mentality. He cites Theroux (1986) as explaining how locals often expect 'home plus' when they go abroad: 'home plus fish and chips' or 'home plus a supermarket' (now a reality with corporate expansionism, where Tesco, Walmart and McDonalds are virtually everywhere: see Ritzer 2008 on the McDonaldisation of society). Locals do not see the need to change their attitudes whereas cosmopolitans do: they see everywhere potentially as home; they are happy to internalise the cultures they find themselves in. These ideas can be helpful for theorising your practices with others in all contexts.

Their relevance for action research are best articulated by Kemmis (2009) and Kemmis and Heikkinen (2012), about the interrelated nature of our 'sayings, doings and relatings' through ecologies of practice. They say that practices are living things, grounded in existing cultural–discursive, material–economic, discursive and social–political conditions (Kemmis and Heikkinen 2012). But it all depends on your personal ontological positioning and how you see and treat others.

THE USES OF CHANGE

The ideas here are developed in Chapter 8, about developing learning organisations. This is where your contribution as a researcher and theorist is crucial. It has special relevance for living in a world of increasing global interconnectedness. People can learn from and with you, and find new ways of developing sales as a dialogical practice with people at its heart, rather than only product-focused or market-driven. There is no argument about the fact that selling is about making a living; what is at issue is how we do it and how the sales encounter can lead to an enhanced sense of wellbeing for all.

This returns us to Chapter 1. Probably the most important (and most difficult) task is to critique your own practices and thinking. This can be difficult, because it involves critiquing your system of thinking while using that same system of thinking. However, it is essential if we are serious about influencing processes of personal and social transformation. Action research could be one of the few methodologies that require this as a core feature.

This brings us to Chapter 3, where we discuss how sales and action research come together, and why salespeople should consider researching their practices in the first place.

Summary

This chapter has explored a range of ideas about action research: specifically, what it is, who can do it, how to do it and where it came from. It outlines some of the underpinning assumptions of action research, especially those to do with ontological, epistemological, methodological and social commitments. Action research is about changing social situations, which begins with people changing their own thinking. To change one's thinking, however, can be difficult because it means becoming critical of the system of thinking itself, and this itself is a core feature of action research. This idea is further developed in Chapter 3, which is about why salespeople should do action research.

Chapter 3

Why Should Salespeople do Action Research?

This chapter explains why you should do research, and why action research in particular. Doing research involves knowing about different forms of research so you can choose a particular kind. Action research can help you improve your practice, contribute to the professionalisation of sales, realise your values and help others realise theirs. You can make your contributions to practice and policy debates by drawing on your knowledge and experience.

The chapter covers the following:

- Why should you do research?

- Why should you do action research?

- What does returning to study involve?

Why Should You Do Research?

The main reasons why you should do research are to:

- improve your practice;

- show you are a competent professional;

- show you are a competent researcher and theorist.

IMPROVING YOUR PRACTICE

Improving sales involves finding ways to ensure the quality of customer experience as the basis of increasing sales, that is, researching how to do it.

Research is always associated with learning: that is, acquiring or creating new knowledge. According to Habermas (1975: 15) we cannot *not* learn in processes of social evolution; Foucault (1980) says that knowledge is power. There are different forms of learning, including stimulus response and constructivist forms, learning from books, from other people, and from your own experience. The question is, which kinds are most relevant to improving sales?

The philosopher John Dewey's ideas are important. He saw learning as a process of inquiry where people actively engage with their experience in their social and socio-economic worlds, and the world of ideas and concepts. Learning from experience leads to increased knowledge of these worlds. You do this in sales: you acquire different kinds of knowledge in different ways. You learn how to sell through practical experience and you learn theoretical ideas through reading or listening to others. Dewey saw experience as active first-hand engagement. Learning is purposeful, not necessarily for a concrete outcome but for more and better learning. This perspective is different from theorists such as Kolb (1984), who saw experience as in the past. Dewey saw experience as in the present, so learning is always future-oriented. Feynman agrees. He says, 'Knowledge has no real value if all you can tell me is what happened yesterday' (1999: 25). We need knowledge for today that helps shape our futures.

The ideas also highlight the need for focus (see Senge et al. 2005 and page 55), that is, being fully present in the current situation: Varga (2009) also writes about the need for focused inquiry in business settings. The highest form of focus is 'flow' (Csikszentmihalyi 1990), when you become immersed in the activity: you become part of it and it becomes part of you. Sales also involves focused concentration and commitment.

Dewey was a direct forerunner of action research, though he did not call it this. For him, learning from experience took the form:

- experiencing a perplexing situation because habitual actions are no longer working;

- clarifying and defining the problem;

- inquiring into the situation and formulating a tentative hypothesis about a possible solution;

- testing the hypothesis in action and revising through rigorous tests;

- understanding the current situation better and acting on the solution (see Elkjaer, 2009: 76).

This typology is reflected in the processes of sales and of action research (see below). It links with other theoretical frameworks such as Mezirow's transformative learning theory, as follows:

- a disorienting dilemma;

- self-examination with feelings of fear, anger, guilt or shame;

- a critical assessment of assumptions;

- recognition that one's discontent and the process of transformation are shared;

- exploration of options for new roles, relationships and actions;

- planning a course of action;

- acquiring knowledge and skills for implementing one's plans;

- provisional trying of new roles;

- building competence and self-confidence in new roles and relationships;

- a reintegration into one's life on the basis of conditions dictated by one's new perspective (Mezirow 2009: 94).

Self-reflection is central. The greatest challenge, Dewey felt, was to avoid a descent into dogmatism. This could be achieved through critique. Dewey's work also laid the foundations for the work of Schön (1983), and his ideas about the reflective practitioner. Reflective practice has 'implications for the professional's relation to his [sic] clients, for the organizational settings of practice, for the future interaction of research and practice, and for the place of the professions in the larger society' (Schön 1983: ix).

Schön draws on the idea of tacit knowledge, developed by theorists such as Polanyi (1958), saying that 'the competent practitioner usually knows more than they can say. They exhibit a kind of knowing-in-practice, most of which is tacit' (Schön 1983: viii). The task of research is to help the practitioner make this knowledge explicit and explain its contribution to enhancing practices and personal and social wellbeing.

Also relevant to sales research are the ideas of Argyris (1964, 1993), about how practitioners' theories of action can contribute to enhanced organisational learning. Argyris and Schön (1978, 1996) developed the idea of 'single loop', 'double loop' and 'triple loop' learning. Single loop learning is when we respond to immediate situations and imagine solutions. Say your customer contacts you to complain that the furniture they purchased has not arrived on schedule, so you contact your company to find out the reasons for the delay: you acquire information and act on it. Double loop learning refers to questioning the underlying conditions that led to the situation in the first place. Your company explains that the schedule you negotiated with your customer was too tight, and you had not checked with your company whether your negotiated delivery time was realistic. You learn to check in future with the company before arranging delivery dates. Triple loop learning is about learning to learn from reflections on experiences. You talk with your company about the need for salespeople to be aware of the importance of good communication with all departments. Everyone learns together from one another's experiences (see more in Chapter 8).

There is a large literature on reflective practice (for example, Bolton 2010; Ghaye 2011; Moon 2010). It links with related literatures about situated learning (Lave and Wenger 1991), lifelong learning (Field 2006; Schuller and Watson 2009), workplace learning (Garnett et al. 2009), communities of inquiry (Garrison 2011) and communities of practice (Wenger 1999). All these literatures emphasise the need for continual lifelong learning. Implications for you are that if you are not learning you are actually going backwards because you are falling behind your competitors, who are intent on learning.

SHOWING THAT YOU ARE A COMPETENT PROFESSIONAL

It is important for you, your customers and your profession to show that you are a competent professional. This means knowing how professionalism is currently understood.

Traditionally, professionalism in sales has been theorised in terms of personal and context-specific characteristics, including:

- specialised knowledge, including practical knowledge;

- reliability;

- image;

- enthusiasm;

- autonomy;

- care for clients;

- etiquette, courtesy and respect, interpersonal relationships, listening;

- preparation and follow-up;

- communication;

- self-confidence, self-awareness, self-discipline;

- competence;

- ethical attitudes, honesty and integrity;

- self-regulation, initiative, time management;

- poise;

- accountability.

Most sales manuals say you must live up to characteristics like these for maximum success. The idea stems from a trait theory of personality, developed by Allport (1961), Cattell (1965) and others, outlining specific characteristics relevant to different situations. It also led to a large literature about personality types (for example, Eysenck 1971), which was often used for job selection – a rather questionable practice, since identifying specific types often factors out people's individuality and their capacity to re-create themselves according to personal visions.

In the 1970s, Hoyle (1975) extended debates by suggesting two kinds of professionalism:

1.   'professionalism', which refers mainly to the characteristics of a professional (outlined above), and becomes a form of 'restricted professionalism';

2.   'professionality', involving 'extended professionalism', referring to the knowledge, skills and procedures developed through experience of practices.

These ideas have been developed by others, including Evans (2008) who speaks about 'enacted professionalism'. This is when practitioners demonstrate in practice their desire to live up to their own (and possibly others') expectations. The ideas are important for salespeople for the following reasons.

Currently the sales literatures emphasise professional expertise as knowing the skills of the job, the 'tricks of the trade', rather than knowing the trade itself. Some texts take an anthropological view (Delves Broughton 2012), related to trait theory, outlining the characteristics and strategies of well-known salespeople as models of good practice. This approach can be helpful but limited, as it reinforces the idea of applying other people's theories to practice rather than creating one's own. It also does not acknowledge that learning the craft of selling means undertaking an apprenticeship of committed text-based and field-based study and raising to conscious awareness the knowledge acquired through experience (Sennett 2008: see above page 61); and that extended professionalism involves demonstrating responsibility and accountability to others and self. Becoming an extended professional involves research into practice, with clearly identified aims of contributing to the wellbeing of the end-user (McDonnell and McNiff, in preparation).

As professionals we should be able to say, 'I am good at my job'; if we cannot say this we ought not to be doing the job. Saying this will inspire other people to have confidence in you and is a first step to success. This all means you need to stay on top of what you are doing to ensure you are doing it well, regularly evaluating your practice, checking what is going well and addressing those elements that are not going so well. Collecting research data enables you to see what is really happening rather than what you think is happening.

SHOWING THAT YOU ARE A COMPETENT RESEARCHER AND THEORIST

Developing research capacity and competence means learning basic research principles in order to:

- meet the expectations of professional bodies;

- contribute to knowledge of sales practice and theory.

Meeting the expectations of professional bodies

Many professions require practitioners to engage in on-the-job professional learning, usually termed continuing professional development (CPD) or continuing professional education (CPE). Some professions such as nursing and podiatry expect this as a form of accreditation: you must produce evidence of CPD to continue your registration. No requirement currently exists for salespeople. CPD tends to take the form of attending company briefings or in-house professional education courses. Salespeople's professionalism is judged mainly by numbers of sales and returning customers. This distorted view does not do justice to the professional knowledge of practitioners, which leads to sales being seen as a job but not a profession. It is assumed that anyone can sell. Success is seen as achieved by reciting a pre-recorded script or copying more experienced practitioners.

Contributing to knowledge of sales practice and theory

To establish direct selling as a profession, practitioners themselves need to develop its theoretical base. Currently research tends to be done by academics who produce scholarly articles written from a propositional, abstract perspective, often unrelated to the real-life experiences of salespeople. Salespeople are not required or seen as able to do research, nor is practical theory always recognised. There is less emphasis on the need for inquiry (in Dewey's sense), or critically reflective practice for improving practices through learning. Theory of sales usually emanates from academies and boardrooms. In Chapter 8 we suggest that universities could learn much from salespeople, given that universities have themselves become businesses, and academics find themselves positioned as inexperienced salespeople; experienced salespeople could in fact teach academics how to do the job. First, however, they need to produce an evidence base to show how they do the job themselves and show what it means to be an extended sales professional. They explain how they hold themselves accountable for what they are doing and why they are doing it.

So how can action research help you?

SELLING AND ITS COMPLEXITIES

My name is Suzanne and I sell office equipment to small and medium-sized enterprises. After reading *The Reflective Practitioner* by Donald Schön I decided to look beneath the surface of my sales activity to identify which ethical, philosophical, professional and cultural values informed my practice. This made me realise what a complex area sales is. Some of the underlying conflicts between colleagues' different values systems would show up when we went for a beer in the evening and discussed issues such as what selling is about.

My manager was a larger-than-life consummate professional. He had worked hard and accumulated wealth. This wealth had been reduced considerably over three divorces and he had little contact with his children. He was a hard-driving boss who nevertheless emphasised that there was no need to sell unethically. He said you should be able to meet any one of your customers in the street and look them in the eye.

Another colleague was a devoted family man who said his one aim was to send all his children to university. This chap was regularly in disputes with the manager through being caught out in sharp practices and unethical behaviour. Senior directors would not let the manager fire him because he made a good contribution to profits.

We all agreed on our frustration at being called into strategy meetings to be told the latest approach to selling. We would then be given targets based on forecasts. These approaches and targets would follow advice by strategic sales or marketing consultants without any input from us. We asked ourselves who owned the knowledge of sales in our company and why it was assumed that the people who actually did the selling could not understand it.

These kinds of experiences and episodes reinforce that, for me, the best approach to a life in sales seems to be to interrogate one's underlying values and try to live by them in order to live in harmony with oneself.

Why Should You Do Action Research?

Action research is real-world research (Robson 2011). It is practical, purposeful (Elliott 1991) and workplace-based (Garnett et al. 2009). It is also highly rigorous and ethical (Reason and Bradbury 2008); this is also an internationally agreed criterion of continuing and higher education. This is good news for salespeople, who tend to be pro-active, self-sufficient and future-oriented as part of their jobs. Doing action research requires innovative and creative thinking to imagine new futures and realise them. Action research becomes an effective form of research for sales: it is action for human and environmental betterment.

Appreciating why you should do action research rather than traditional social science research means knowing the differences between different research paradigms so you can justify your choice. A paradigm refers to different approaches and sets of ideas and what they stand for, that is, their purposes. This means considering two issues:

1.   ideas about different forms of research;

2.   ideas about human interests.

FORMS OF RESEARCH

Many literatures, including seminal work by Carr and Kemmis (1986) organise the field into:

- empirical research;

- interpretive research;

- critical theory research;

- newer forms arising out of critical theory, including action research.

Empirical research

This form of research is used when a researcher wishes to gather information about a situation, so they can see what is going on and make suggestions about how to control it through manipulating variables. Positioning yourself as an empirical researcher means distancing yourself from the situation you are studying, usually as an outsider researcher, and investigating it. People in the situation are often seen as data to show what is happening. Data gathering tends to be quantitative (how many people did certain things), though qualitative data may also be gathered (how well and to what extent they did those things). This form of research and researcher positionality is common in the orthodox social sciences (such as psychology, sociology and management). It can be used in action research, perhaps during a reconnaissance or evaluation phase. The aim is largely to demonstrate a cause and effect relationship ('If I do x, then y will happen') in order to predict and control what will happen in the future. In an overall empirical research design, the usual criteria for judging quality and rigour are whether the research is replicable (an experiment carried out using the same methodology will yield the same results as the original), generalisable (the results may be generalised to similar situations), and objective (values, emotions or beliefs are excluded so the research remains value free). You could use this kind of research if, say, you wished to show trends in sales practices, or show increases in numbers of appointments as part of an evaluation.

Interpretive research

This kind of research is used to get a deeper understanding of what is happening in social situations. A researcher's positioning varies from being an outsider researcher investigating the situation from an externalist perspective, to an insider researcher, working as part of the group you are studying, and different stances between (see page 38). The aim is to gather data and generate evidence to show the development of ideas and practices and give reasons why they are happening. You could use this approach, say, to explain how collaborative working rather than allocating tasks to individuals can lead to organisational success. Your report would include the voices of colleagues and other research participants.

Critical research (also called 'critical theoretic research')

Critical theory was a powerful movement that began in the 1920s and 1930s, stemming from concerns that said it was sufficient only to observe and interpret what was happening in the social world. Critical theorists maintained that it was also necessary to analyse why it was happening and how individuals were part of a social situation. For example, if you felt your sales figures needed to be higher, you could ask, 'What am I doing that is leading to lower sales than expected?' or, 'Is it time to change my product or pursue another market?' Critical theory calls for researchers to demonstrate critical understanding of contextualising cultural, political and historical factors. It involves critique, the ability to appreciate the underlying and public messages of social situations. Underlying messages are unspoken: they become absorbed into the culture, and people internalise them and even become convinced that they were their ideas in the first place (see Foucault 1980).

Action research

Action research was influenced by critical theory, as well as other social movements and a general post-World War I *zeitgeist* that called for democratic and emancipatory practices – see the work of Paulo Freire (1996), Dewey's ideas of the free schools movement (Miller 2002) and Zinn's ideas about democratic labour movements (2005). Action research went beyond critical theory. Action researchers maintain that it is not enough only to gather empirical data, understand what is happening, or adopt a critical stance to a social situation: they also need to take action to change it. Action research has always involved the idea of changing and improving practices through improving understanding. While there are currently different approaches to action research, this idea remains constant.

No one kind of research is 'better' than another. They are all different and used at different points for different purposes. Sometimes people mix methodologies, a 'mixed methodology' approach. You can also adopt a 'mixed-methods' approach using different forms of data gathering and analysis. If you used a mixed-methodologies approach, you could, for example, use an empirical approach to gather information about a particular aspect as part of a wider action research approach aimed at improvement. You would use the data to assess what was needed and speculate whether it would work.

However, choice of research methodology is also informed by what you wish to achieve. This brings us to the idea of human interests.

IDEAS ABOUT HUMAN INTERESTS

Jürgen Habermas, a widely respected social scientist, developed ideas about how knowledge and action are always linked with and informed by purposes. This is an essential element of sales where you need to check your motivations and whose interests you are serving in a business relationship. Habermas identified three kinds of human interests involved in creating knowledge (doing research): technical, practical and emancipatory (Habermas 1972, 1987). In 2002 (refined in 2013), McNiff added a fourth category of relational–dialogical interests.

- **Technical interests (sometimes called 'work knowledge').** This focuses on the generation of technical rational knowledge (know that), with the aim of controlling the environment. You could manipulate a sales situation to serve your own interests. However, this would not help you ensure a good customer experience, or check whether your behaviour would win you repeat sales. Research is often carried out from a technical perspective to see how well a product is selling, but this is often taken as the basis for judgements about customer satisfaction and can often be misleading in the longer term.

- **Practical interests.** This focuses on meaning making and interpretation, in order to understand the social and political forces that have influenced, or still influence your environment. A customer may judge the quality of a product in terms of how well it served their practical needs, such as choosing between motorboats for best functionality. You could appeal to an elderly customer's practical mobility needs when selling a mobility scooter, or to a family's needs when selling space-saving wardrobes.

- **Emancipatory interests.** Practices and knowledge can be geared towards self-knowledge, and therefore emancipation of others and self. You could take part in your organisational planning to learn better how to react to decisions. In direct selling, you would find ways of enabling customers to choose according to their identified needs.

- **Relational–dialogical interests.** These are about how valuable knowledge may be created through dialogical relationships. This kind of interest is central to developing a new dialogical paradigm in sales (as communicated in this book). You encourage your customer to see the encounter as a joint journey of enquiry.

WHAT ARE WE HERE FOR?

Sally and Terry are partners in a gift shop, where they sell toys, including clockwork ducks. One day a group of children come into the shop and wind up the clockwork ducks for fun. They overwind one of the ducks and break it. They then throw the duck back into its container saying, 'It's no good now: it's broken.' Terry goes over to the children and advises them that they will have to pay for the ducks, and spends a little time explaining why this is so and how they need to develop a more responsible attitude to other people's property. Sally is angry, comes over to the group and shouts at the children and throws them out of the shop. She is also angry at Terry's attitudes and behaviour and says to him, 'Your job is to take their money, not to educate them.'

These ideas about human interests can help you decide which research methodology or methods to choose: social science research tends to prioritise technical rational and practical interests, whereas action research spans practical, emancipatory and relational–dialogical interests. You may well draw on all kinds of interests at different points in all kinds of research.

You can also use this framework to help you decide which behaviours to adopt when selling. You would present the technical benefits of a product to appeal to your client's practical interests, or show how the product would serve their emancipatory interests by freeing them up to do other things. You would adopt a relational perspective throughout to establish the kind of relationship with your customer that is going to lead to more referrals and repeat orders.

Why Do Action Research?

This section focuses on how doing action research can help your sales practice, as follows:

- action research and work-based learning;

- self-evaluation for improving practice;

- professional development and appraisal;

- action research and the new knowledge economy.

ACTION RESEARCH AND WORK-BASED LEARNING

There is now a considerable literature on work-based learning, emphasising the centrality of practitioners' research for improving their own practices. Many university courses included a practicum or work experience module. Of particular relevance is the idea of Mode 1, Mode 2 and Mode 3 knowledge.

Mode 1 knowledge (Gibbons et al. 1994) is seen as produced primarily within disciplines and usually in higher education institutions or at boardroom level. Established disciplinary and institutional boundaries dictate who can contribute and who judges the quality of the knowledge produced. Mode 2 knowledge is problem-based, interdisciplinary, and created through discussion and negotiation. It is socially oriented, created by practitioners for other practitioners and citizens. Barnett (2004) critiques both Mode 1 and Mode 2 forms as too limiting, because, he says, they often suppose that solutions to problems exist and may be found; the knowledge created is too specific and bounded. He proposes Mode 3 forms of knowledge, about practitioners' active knowing and learning within uncertainty. Mode 3 knowledge is about the whole person, when we find our own resources, often collaboratively, to find appropriate ways of living together.

Ideas about knowledge and its uses are often termed 'knowledge management', and are relevant for new forms of organisational practices. Action research is a powerful methodology for this, emphasising ideas about creative learning and collaborative working, grounded in personal and collective values. Action researchers do not aim for a stable state or ideal solution, because these do not exist. Instead they recognise that emerging ideas and claims are always best guess and check they are not simply reinforcing their prejudices or ignoring data that show things going in directions they had not anticipated.

SELF-EVALUATION FOR IMPROVING PRACTICE

Part of work-based learning is self-evaluation. Traditional views of professional education see knowledge as belonging to an expert, and many organisations bring in consultants to help their workforces. The consultants' job is often to evaluate organisational practices and provide feedback to inform improvements. This is fine, provided it acts as the beginning of a longer-term project where all practitioners are encouraged to accept responsibility for their own professional learning. The job of the consultant then changes to provider of intellectual and emotional support rather than as expert with all the answers.

Self-evaluation is part of ongoing professionalism. You decide how you are going to sell, whether in a manipulative way or honestly and with integrity, according to whichever interests are influencing your decisions, and can account for what you do and decide. Self-evaluation helps you check whether you are realising your values and are prepared to negotiate these in relation to those of your customers and colleagues. This capacity to negotiate values and work out strategies for accommodating all perspectives is an essential aspect of professionalism, in sales and all professions. This capacity for negotiating values could be considered as a criterion for judging quality in research and practice (see Chapter 7).

ACTION RESEARCH AND THE NEW KNOWLEDGE ECONOMY

Especially relevant to sales is how your action research can contribute to a new knowledge economy. Many governments promote the idea of wider access, which means that more people have the opportunity of undertaking continuing and higher education. More business and industry managers require higher education institutions to 'produce' graduates with practical skills relevant to the production of new technologies and new forms of consumer goods. It is also recognised that physical resources such as oil and gas will run out soon, so the need to switch from a resources-based economy to a knowledge economy is pressing. This means that practitioners from all walks of life need to create new forms of resources and goods to sustain an increasing world population. It also carries imperatives for business to develop awareness of its environmental impact. Business practices account for massive environmental damage (Hawken 2010) and you are part of this. And what about fair working conditions for all? The concept of Fair Trade is well known, but not everyone thinks about the distribution of Fair Trade goods, whether through a small shop or a large retailer. Who do you buy from and sell to? How do you develop your knowledge to influence new business working practices that will nurture the environment, ensure fair working practices, and contribute to a world in which your children will be able to work?

PROFESSIONAL ASSESSMENT AND APPRAISAL

This shift towards insider knowledge and expertise has led to changes in forms of professional appraisal. Many work-based and continuing and higher education courses use incremental learning and formative evaluation methods. This means you can build on previous learning through developing your existing knowledge of practice. Your professional portfolio shows the development of understanding and learning and its uses for personal and social wellbeing.

You assume responsibility for your own practices and capacity to explain them. You become authorised to make judgements about your own professionality, grounding those judgements in a validated evidence base available to the critical scrutiny of organisational peers and the general public. You do this through producing work-based reports such as company memos and other forms of communication including social media. Building up your professional profile on Facebook or LinkedIn or through your personal or company website can help raise your credibility in the public domain, and win you more customers. This communicates that you know what you are doing.

Producing your evidence base shows you as a person to be trusted. This kind of publicly accountable professionalism can help raise the status of selling as a profession too, and does away with stereotypical images of salespersons as fast talkers in sharp suits.

We now discuss some of the main issues involved in returning to study.

What Does Returning to Study Involve?

Action research can be a brilliant means for returning to study. Study can take the form of courses for work-based CPD and formal continuing and higher degree work. Getting accreditation means registering on a continuing or higher degree course. Course attendance requirements and study patterns vary and can include organised study sessions and informal networking with peers and supervisors. Home-based study is commonplace, with assignments submitted as part of coursework.

Many people find the experience of returning to study exhilarating while others find it intimidating, possibly because of largely defunct images of authoritarian teachers and rigid structures. This is no longer a reality for most contexts (though it is in some). Many academic staff are required to act as professional educators and supporters, as well as have expert subject-based or disciplines-based knowledge. Many have first-hand experience of supported learning, since they are required to undertake CPD themselves, supported by professional developers. Action research is frequently a chosen methodology.

Returning to study has personal, professional and practical implications for you, and you need to decide if you are willing to accept them. You can find good advice in resources such as Dawson (2005), and most institutions offer online personalised help. Here are some of the most common implications to consider.

PERSONAL IMPLICATIONS

A change in self-image

Returning to learning can mean changing your self-image; you become an adult learner as well as a salesperson. This often involves a change in form of discourse: when you are in a selling situation you speak the language of sales, whereas in a learning context you speak the language of learning and professional development. You become an academic and learn an academic language. Many practitioners speak a language in the workplace that gives descriptions of actions (we did this, they did that; we sold 100 units; our company AGM took place last week). Academic language is more analytical and offers explanations for actions (we developed a new policy about cold calling acting on empirical evidence; 200 units represents a significant advance in sales; the AGM brings people together and enables them to communicate). The aim of researching in action is to produce both descriptions and explanations of practice; explanation is a main currency in higher education. You have to develop your researcher's voice, which is probably different from your salesperson's voice. This can be done with practice and conscious intent. Some people pick it up easily while others have to work at it.

Reading

Be prepared to read academic and philosophical texts. This means in-depth reading. Aim to make notes as you read and engage critically with the ideas, that is, not take them at face value but interrogate and possibly challenge what you are reading and keep records of your learning. The text represents another person's voice; you are encouraged to agree or disagree with them, and say why. In-depth reading can be time consuming: some authors pack a lot into sentences, while others write in an accessible way. Your course tutor will give you summaries and handouts but these are shortcuts and no substitute for the real thing. Your tutor will give you advice about which texts to read and how to use the ideas to support your studies.

Be prepared to say you don't know

Learning means finding out something new, which means acknowledging that you do not know it already. Some people find it hard to say this, especially executives, who feel they are expected to know everything. Lack of knowledge is seen as a sign of vulnerability, whereas it should be seen as a sign of strength where you are willing to engage with learning.

Always ask if you do not understand something. Staff are there to help and provide resources. Use whatever sources of knowledge you have to find out what you need: course and workplace colleagues, the Internet, social networking, libraries and resource banks. Develop networks and attend study groups. Share your reading with family and friends and get their critical reflections on ideas. They can provide insights that will help you develop your knowledge. Avail of existing chat rooms or set one up yourself. All kinds of resources are available and accessible.

Progressive companies provide forums where practitioners can share their ideas and get critical feedback from colleagues through presenting regular progress reports at staff meetings. This would be an expectation if the company is funding you. Getting colleagues' (and customers') feedback is an excellent way to test the validity of your ideas and strengthen them.

Be prepared to spend time on study

One of the problem areas in returning to adult study is the difficulty of finding time and space within an already busy schedule, while trying to balance work and family commitments. It is one of the most common factors in dropout rates. Yet you need to do it if you wish to succeed. Before you commit to a course ask yourself what you are prepared to put out of your life in order to put the course in. Are you prepared to forgo the match on Saturday or your favourite television soap? You cannot have everything; as a salesperson you know better than others that things comes with a price. What are you prepared to pay? Do not avoid this issue: it can make or break a commitment to study.

PROFESSIONAL IMPLICATIONS

As well as requiring personal commitment, a return to learning requires professional commitment to exploring ideas, including the following.

Which kind of knowledge?

Think about which kind of knowledge is worth having, how you are going to acquire and use it. Do you need to develop your practical skills and competences, your subject knowledge, your personal knowledge and wisdom? Possibly all? Think about who can help you and how your relationship can be managed. Will it involve attending further study sessions, using external resources? To what extent will your current workplace provide these? How collaborative will colleagues be? Is a learning culture already in place, and if not, will you be allowed to develop one? Think how long it took for Andy Dufresne to set up a learning culture in *The Shawshank Redemption*, but he did it eventually.

Developing an attitude of critical reflection

Harland and Pickering (2011) speak about the need to develop values pluralism, a willingness to accept that other people think in their own ways and value certain things that you do not. Learning to appreciate that not everyone thinks and acts the same as you can be difficult. Undertaking higher study involves developing a critical attitude to your own thinking as well as others'. You develop critical literacy (Lankshear and Knobel 2011) where you are able to engage with public discourses and explain the historical and cultural circumstances that have led to views and opinions. You have to be prepared for such engagement so you can defend your own position with justification, otherwise you could be seen as arguing from a position of thoughtlessness.

Use knowledge wisely not recklessly

Think about why you are acquiring knowledge and how you are going to use it once you have it. Will you use it wisely to become, say, an academic citizen (Macfarlane 2007) who is committed to the virtue of service, or use it recklessly, as countless people do to further their own ends? Lilla (2001) describes Heidegger as squandering his considerable intellectual powers by committing them to the Nazi regime. A higher education award is held as a licence to practice, a distinctive privilege. It is your responsibility to use it well.

Learn to write

No two ways about it, study programmes require you to write, whether for assignments, dissertations and theses or company proposals, reports and websites. Learning to write is different from learning about content. Many people find their work does not receive full acknowledgement if they fail to communicate appropriately with their readers. Many return-to-study programmes offer support in writing, and you should avail of them. Learn correct grammar, punctuation and spelling, how to link ideas and construct paragraphs, and put them together as a well-formed text. This does not happen overnight. Like everything, writing expertise requires a small amount of talent and a lot of hard work. You simply have to get on with it: do the work, as Pressfield (2011) says. It is easy to find excuses; don't even look for them but just get on and do it.

As well as these personal professional implications there are also implications for organisational learning, which is where you can exercise your educational influence, learnt from experience. Some of these are explored further in Chapter 8.

PRACTICAL IMPLICATIONS

Think about the following practical issues.

Support of family and workplace colleagues

Negotiate time and space with family, friends and workplace colleagues, when they will allow you to study and perhaps help. They can do some reading for you and give you summaries; they can act as research assistants and write up your notes or transcribe recorded conversations. Doing this as a family can be fun. Soliciting the support of colleagues can have unexpected consequences. As well as refusals, you can also get enthusiastic offers to become critical friends and study companions. Your manager may prove to be an ally, ready to accompany you on sales visits to observe you in action and give you critical feedback. You may even get some remission of time from work.

Resources

Have you appropriate and sufficient resources to support your study programme? Do you need to attend conferences, purchase books or get a more powerful computer? Many companies offer such resources, often expecting a return on their investment by some kind of additional work or commitment to long-term loyalty. Your most important resources are your internal ones, such as being able to see a job through to a high standard. This requires you honestly to take stock of your own capacity for excellence, including attending courses, handing in work on time and keeping yourself in good order throughout. It requires learning to work with others, including your supervisor, taking advice and not objecting if it initially appears wrong-headed, and learning to negotiate. You need the same skills to negotiate with colleagues as with customers: the capacity for listening, dialogue, self-critique and determination. You also need the courage of your own convictions and a refusal to give up or diminish your own ideas. These may be the same skills and knowledge capacities as those it takes to sell. Whatever they may be, you have them in abundance. It is your responsibility to develop them and use them well.

Summary

This chapter outlines reasons why you should do action research into your sales practice. Key reasons given are to improve your practice, which means increasing your sales effectiveness. You also need to show that you are a competent professional: this is essential in a competitive world. It is also important to show that you are a competent lifelong learner, researcher and theorist, so that sales is seen as an evidence-based profession.

We now move to Part II, which gives advice about how to research your sales practice in action.

PART II
Doing Action Research in Sales

This Part is about the practicalities of doing action research in sales, where you integrate research, action and theory. You learn about your practice of selling through learning how to research it, and you can explain more adequately what you are doing. As you become better at researching your practice you become better in the practice and better at explaining. There is no division between learning, doing and explaining.

However, for purposes of analysis and understanding it can be helpful to look at the two processes of action research and selling separately, to see how they link together. This is what we do in the next four chapters. This kind of analysis can be especially helpful if you are looking at your studies as a project. Most courses on workplace and higher degree programmes ask you to do a project, so these kinds of analyses can help you manage your project systematically and draw up appropriate strategies for action. However, remember always to keep it in perspective and see the overall processes as integrated.

Also for purposes of analysis, we present the processes of action research and selling as stages. Each stage has its own internal order and logical sequence. The sequence tends to be linear: you do things in order. In real life you may find there are many overlaps and detours because of other factors, but it is important to try to maintain the sequence to keep the experience of doing the project coherent. Analysing your practice like this enables you to explain it to others.

Different project management texts have different ideas about the main stages in a research project. We suggest the following:

- designing and planning your project (this phase is sometimes is called 'concept planning' or 'conceptualising');

- strategic action planning: drawing up action plans and imagining solutions;

- implementing and doing;

- evaluating, consolidating and developing.

Most sales texts agree that the main stages in a sales project are:

- prospecting, including qualifying;

- connecting and appointing;

- presenting, including closing;

- consolidating and developing.

Remember that each stage of the sales process falls somewhere under the overarching AIDA umbrella (AIDA stands for getting the customer's *attention*; engaging their *interest* in the product; arousing their *desire* to buy; encouraging them to take *action* and purchase).

Chapters 4–7 are organised according to these parallel stages:

Chapter	Stage in your action research project	Stage in your sales project
4	Designing and planning your research project	Prospecting, including qualifying
5	Strategic action planning: drawing up action plans; imagining solutions	Connecting and appointing
6	Implementing and doing: trying out the imagined solutions	Presenting, including closing
7	Evaluating and consolidating: checking that everything is working as anticipated	Developing and consolidating

This kind of analysis can act as a starting point for your project and keep it systematic. You need to understand the parts so you can see how they hang together as a whole.

Chapters 4–7

Here is an outline of Chapters 4–7, organised according to the above.

CHAPTER 4: DESIGNING AND PLANNING: PROSPECTING

- Mapping the territory; what to investigate and why; identifying aims and anticipated outcomes; clarifying the focus of the enquiry; doing an initial stocktake of the situation.

- Thinking about prospecting and qualifying: mapping the territory; who to contact and how to find them; stocktaking and clarifying problems; imagining solutions.

CHAPTER 5: STRATEGIC ACTION PLANNING: CONNECTING AND APPOINTING

- How to manage the project; logistical and ethical aspects; different steps in the enquiry; taking stock and checking feasibility; deciding on a methodology and giving reasons.

- Connecting and appointing; how to manage it; taking stock and imagining solutions; ethics; collecting data and keeping records.

CHAPTER 6: TAKING ACTION AND PRESENTING

- Taking action and trying out possible solutions; what kind of action is involved and why; possible effects and implications of the action.

- Presenting: managing different steps – establishing credibility, identifying needs, creating a desire to buy, negotiating objections, closing the sale.

CHAPTER 7: EVALUATING YOUR RESEARCH: CONSOLIDATING AND DEVELOPING

- Evaluating the action: generating evidence; imagining possible modifications in light of the evaluation.

- Consolidating the sale: asking for referrals; checking company backup; ensuring customer aftercare, developing relationships.

Research processes and sales processes can be seen as cyclical: the end of one cycle transforms into another (Figure 2.1). Consolidating means reflecting on how you have managed the sales process and what you have learnt and may do differently next time. Referrals from existing customers may be the start of a new sales cycle with a new customer, so you could have many sales projects working at different stages. Aim to stay on top of your work by seeing it as a holistic research project.

In Part III we discuss what might be the most significant aspects of doing your research, and how you can communicate the significance to different audiences for specific purposes.

Chapter 4

Designing and Planning: Prospecting

This chapter is about designing and planning your action research project in sales. This involves thinking about its overall concept in terms of what you wish to achieve and how you are going to achieve it. It involves thinking about and deciding on an appropriate methodology.

Designing an action enquiry means first taking stock of your current situation to identify which areas are satisfactory or whether any need improvement. You then have to be realistic about what you can and cannot do. Designing a project itself involves planning, that is, getting an overall picture of what your aims are and how you are going to achieve them. Some literatures refer to this as concept planning, or conceptualising your project. Once you have got this picture you can begin strategic action planning, that is, drawing up detailed plans about what you intend to do. This is dealt with in Chapter 5.

In this chapter we take prospecting as illustrative, because this is the first stage in a sales process and also involves conceptualising and designing your overall sales strategy. The principles of designing and conceptualising apply to both research and sales; both processes are integrated.

The chapter contains these sections.

- What are the principles of designing and conceptualising action research? What does it involve?

- What are the principles of prospecting? What does prospecting involve?

- How do I research prospecting in action?

What Are the Principles of Designing and Conceptualising Action Research? What Does it Involve?

Designing and conceptualising a project focuses on issues of methodology. This means:

- giving a rationale for your project, that is, saying why you are going to do it and what you hope to achieve;

- outlining how you intend to do it, which refers to the procedures and methods you intend to use.

Designing is essential in action research. It involves having a longer-term vision of what you wish to achieve. A first step in achieving it is to take stock of what is happening in your current situation. This means identifying any aspects you think need improving, and why you think this may be the case. This in itself means considering the values that inspire your work and inform your actions.

RESPONDING TO CHANGE

David works in a travel agency and sells transportation and accommodation to people travelling on holiday and business. He has lost some of his existing customers recently, and suspects they have turned to the Internet for the same services as he provides. His concern is to (1) ensure that existing customers maintain their loyalty to him, which means planning how to ensure this, possibly by delivering an enhanced, personalised service and (2) build up his customer base again, which means finding new customers. What to do? His first step is to (1) take stock of how many customers he has lost, find out why they are defecting, and find ways of attracting them back; (2) find new customers to replace those who will probably not return.

Designing an action enquiry means considering a range of factors, including these:

- knowing the difference between methodology and methods;

- considering the values base of how you research your work;

- choosing an appropriate form of action research and deciding on your research positioning;

- deciding on a research issue and research question;

- identifying conceptual and theoretical frameworks;

- considering who the research is for and how they will benefit.

KNOWING THE DIFFERENCE BETWEEN METHODOLOGY AND METHODS

A methodology and a method are different. A methodology refers to the overall approach to a research programme, including research topic and question, rationale, theoretical and conceptual frameworks, data gathering and evaluation. Methods refer to specific techniques, usually in relation to data gathering and analysis such as questionnaires or interviews. Action research and sales share similar methodologies of review, plan, decide how to take action, evaluate outcomes, reflect on the experience and consider how learning from the experience might influence more effective practices.

CONSIDERING THE VALUES BASE OF HOW YOU RESEARCH YOUR WORK

It is possible to research sales using different methodologies. As noted in Chapter 1, most sales research is currently conducted from an empirical perspective, where a researcher observes and records what salespeople are doing, and interprets their behaviours in light of the researcher's criteria. In this case, salespeople become data in a researcher's enquiry. One of the aims of this kind of research is to generate findings that salespeople may find helpful and so apply the theory to their practices; one of its limitations is that it does not acknowledge the values base of sales or research. While this kind of research has its place, salespeople also need to exercise their agency by researching their own practices in action, acknowledging the values base of what they are doing. Questions you therefore need to think about are: What inspires you to work in sales? How does it give further meaning to your life? This gives a general orientation to and rationale for your practices.

To begin, take stock of your perceptions about your different relationships, as follows:

How do you see yourself?

Do a self-inventory. Look in the mirror: who do you see there? Are you confident about your capacity to succeed, or possibly afraid to have a go? Tracy (1996: 121–5) identifies fear of failure and ignorance as the main obstacles to success in anything. In sales, it can be fear of failing to sell by salespeople, and fear of making a mistake by customers. Acceptance of risk is key to overcoming anxiety.

How do you see your customers and colleagues?

How do you see your customers and colleagues? Do you see them as knowledgeable people with whom you are conducting a collaborative enquiry, or as competitors? Are they thinking people who do not want you to sell to them so much as help them get what they need? While the focus of the research is you and your practice, your practice is about how you work with customers and colleagues.

How do you see sales?

How do you see sales – as selling a product or helping people achieve a dream? Are you passionate about your product or is it about making money? Explaining these things to yourself helps you to clarify your motives for how you sell.

How do you see research?

Do you see it as a means to getting a qualification and a possible promotion, or as developing in-depth knowledge about yourself and your field? You probably want both, and clarifying what you hope to achieve can help you to do so.

CHOOSING AN APPROPRIATE FORM OF ACTION RESEARCH AND DECIDING ON YOUR RESEARCH POSITIONING

In Chapter 1 we identified different forms of action research (insider and outsider action research; first, second and third-person action research), all of which involve people evaluating their practices. We suggest that you evaluate your own practice first so that you speak with the authority of experience when you advise others. In sales it is essential to maintain a regular process of self-evaluation (Tracy 1996) to maintain peak performance, which means doing action research. This involves studying and evaluating your own practice, and deciding whether you are doing your work well and how to improve it where necessary.

DECIDING ON A RESEARCH ISSUE AND RESEARCH QUESTION

Starting an action research project means identifying an issue you feel needs investigating; for example:

- My sales figures are falling, so I need to find ways to increase my sales.

- My list of prospects is thin, so I need to find ways of identifying new prospects.

- I have to hunt for data every time my manager asks to see my figures, so I need to manage my data more effectively and be more prepared.

Insider action research questions often take the form, 'How do I ...?' or 'How do we ...?' So, having identified a research issue, you can formulate an appropriate research question like this:

Research issue	Research question
My sales figures are falling	How do I increase my sales figures?
My list of prospects is thin	How do I find new prospects?
I need to hunt for data every time my manager asks to see my figures	How do I manage my data more effectively?

The changing focus of an action enquiry

Remember that your research focus and issue will probably change over time, given that your work contexts are continuously changing. This means your research question will change too. Your issue about increasing sales could change into a new focus, perhaps about managing your growing database of customers, or how to meet their requirements.

As your research focus and question change, you could develop several research cycles and questions (see Figure 4.1). 'How do I increase my sales?' could change into 'How do I manage my sales ledger more effectively?' At a later stage this could possibly develop into, 'How do I organise visits to accommodate all my clients?' Do not attempt to research everything at once: break the overall enquiry into smaller manageable chunks (see Figure 4.1).

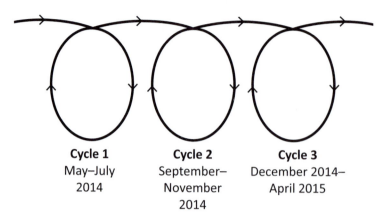

Cycle 1
May–July
2014

Cycle 2
September–
November
2014

Cycle 3
December 2014–
April 2015

Figure 4.1   Continuing action research cycles over time

Cycle 1 May–July 2014

Research issue: I need to find more prospects.

Research question: How do I find more prospects?

Cycle 2 September–November 2014

Research issue: My customer database has grown and I need to find ways of managing the accounts more effectively.

Research question: How do I manage the accounts more effectively?

Cycle 3 December 2014–April 2015

Research issue: I need to organise visits to accommodate all my customers.

How do I organise visits to accommodate all my customers?

You could go on indefinitely pursuing your enquiry; however, you would never reach an end or a final answer. The process could take an emerging transformational form (Figure 4.2).

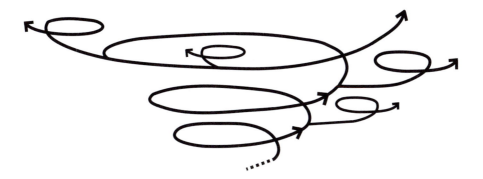

**Figure 4.2   A generative transformational evolutionary process
(McNiff 1984; 2013a)**

Be realistic when choosing your research issue. You cannot do anything about hierarchical organisational structures or a weak economy. You can do something about how you react and find new ways of working. Therefore, when identifying a research issue, keep it small, focused and manageable. Think in terms of the criteria, 'I must do something about this, I can do something about it, and I will do something about it.' In any situation, its what you do next that counts.

KEEPING THE PIPELINE FLOWING

Samira represents a media and publishing company. She has a long list of customers in her area, but she is moving house to a new town about 20 kilometres away. Her dilemma is how to maintain her existing list of customers while building up a clientele in her new district, and how to find new customers to offset the ones she is bound to lose through the move. She is thinking of developing the online features of her work to compensate for the inevitable reduction in face-to-face opportunities.

Remember that action research never comes to closure. As soon as you get to what appears to be the end of a cycle or project, a new one begins. Said (1997) speaks about new beginnings: each moment is a new beginning that holds opportunities for a new future. Arendt (1958) says that the fact that we are born signals an opportunity for a new contribution on earth. These ideas are useful to the world of sales, where nothing stands still, including yourself.

Thinking about your values: why have you chosen this issue?

A great way to begin an action enquiry is to think of your values. Values are the things you believe in and that give your life meaning. What inspires your work in selling? Clearly you need to make a living, but money is not the main value for many salespeople. According to Seligman (2011), the greatest good is happiness and a sense of wellbeing; for Fromm (1956) it is productive work and loving relationships. Most people see money as providing the means towards greater happiness. Some see money as the measure of their constant need to win. The values that inspire selling may also be the desire to contribute to someone else's wellbeing by providing a service or a product or a pleasant buying experience that gives greater value-added to the product. It may also be about raising your own self-esteem and actualising your potentials for living in the social world.

Often salespeople do not stop to think about their values, but doing so is the basis of action research, contrary to traditional forms of scientific and some social scientific research, which see values as contaminating the research process. In action research your values act both as guiding principles to action, and as criteria to judge the quality of the action. This idea is especially important when gathering data and generating evidence. Say perseverance is a key value for you. You aim to persevere when prospecting in spite of setbacks. You could say that achieving a high number of contacts was because of your perseverance. Your value of perseverance now stands as a criterion by which you judge the quality of your practice.

However, you may not always live according to your values. You may prefer to watch cricket on television and deny your value of perseverance. At other times, wider contexts may deny your values. You may work in an organisation or system with values contrary to your own. Habermas (1976) speaks about 'systems' and 'lifeworlds'. Systems are to do with rules, regulations and institutions. Lifeworlds are about people, practices and collaborative living. Habermas says that people often forget they create their own systems: the system takes on a life of its own and becomes separated from the people who create it. People then say, 'Blame the system', which is a good way of shifting responsibility. The system can be a great place to hide.

Also remember that you are not the only person in the selling/purchasing relationship. Your customer and colleagues are also participants, and they have their values. These values may be product-oriented (they know what they want from the product) and relationship-oriented (they know how they would like to be sold to). This brings dilemmas. How do you find ways of negotiating your customer's and your own values? This emphasises the need for dialogue, as a form of negotiation and as a form of coming to mutual understanding.

IDENTIFYING CONCEPTUAL AND THEORETICAL FRAMEWORKS

Conceptual and theoretical frameworks refer to the key concepts that inform your research: for example, good relationships and high-quality service. Researching sales means linking concepts with the literatures. Watkinson (2013) identifies good service as the basis of customer relations; Kahneman and Tversky (2000) speak about strengthening awareness in how we make judgements, as do Argyris and Schön (1996) who focus on understanding frames of reference when making judgements. The identification of conceptual and theoretical frameworks can provide the reasons and explanations for your research and highlights the need to engage with appropriate literatures in formal studies.

An important framework for action research is appreciative inquiry, an idea developed by Cooperrider (Cooperrider et al. 2008) who says that research should be about appreciating what is going well. Adopting an appreciative stance means that instead of asking, 'What is going wrong and how do I put it right?' you begin an enquiry by asking, 'What is going well and how do I account for it?' In researching your sales practices you could look for situations that have gone well and learn from them rather than look for negative ones.

CONSIDERING WHO THE RESEARCH IS FOR AND HOW THEY WILL BENEFIT

Before embarking on any research programme you need to think why you are doing it, who the research is for and if and how they will benefit. An interesting story is told by Sennett (2008: 1–2) about a chance meeting with his former tutor, Hannah Arendt. He writes:

> It was freezing cold on the New York street, but Arendt was oblivious. She wanted me to draw the right lesson: people who make things usually don't understand what they are doing (p. 1).

Arendt went on to remind him of the story of Pandora, the Greek goddess of invention. When Pandora opened her gods-given casket she released the evils of the world as well as its wonders. This, say Arendt and Sennett, is one of the problems of doing research. When the products and findings of the research are sweet, it is easy to forget the effects of the research on human lives and costs. This has implications for you and sales. It is possible to sell virtually anything to anyone. Delves Broughton (2012) explains how, in the Garden of Eden, the snake sold Eve on the idea of eating the apple, without encouraging her to consider the consequences. He continues:

> But from a sales perspective, one has to admire the serpent's hustle. No longer did Eve regard the tree as deadly, but rather as the attractive bearer of tasty fruit, which had the additional effect of making her wise. The serpent was a master of the one-off sale (p. 10).

It depends on your perspective whether you are prepared to sell from an unethical stand or whether you think about the potential consequences. We all make things: we make our lives. When it comes to researching your practices, you have to make your own decisions about your reasons and purposes. Do you develop your conversational skills to make people buy your product or to help them to decide whether to buy it? This was one of the main points in Habermas's ideas of human interests (Chapter 3). In whose interests do we do things? Whose interests do we serve?

In research, as in everyday practices, we should think about what we are doing and why we are doing it. Appreciating fully why you are doing it and what some of the potential consequences may be is core to designing and conceptualising your research.

So, having considered some of the issues involved in designing and conceptualising an action enquiry we now turn to how they play out in the early stages of a sales process. We take prospecting as an example, as the design stage in planning your longer-term sales strategy. First we discuss the principles of prospecting, and then consider how action research and selling come together as a process of enquiry in action.

What Are the Principles of Prospecting? What Does Prospecting Involve?

First, think about what are commonly seen as the aims and anticipated outcomes of prospecting.

AIMS OF PROSPECTING

The aims of prospecting are to find new prospects to ensure a full portfolio of customers to keep you in business on a continual basis. As you are consolidating existing sales you are already looking for new ones and establishing relationships. You also qualify these prospects to check whether they are worth pursuing as viable potential customers.

ANTICIPATED OUTCOMES OF PROSPECTING

You anticipate that you will recruit as many customers as you can handle. Properly handled, existing customers may recommend you to new ones, so your customers will do some of your prospecting for you.

Now think about the commonly agreed principles of prospecting.

THE PRINCIPLES OF PROSPECTING

Prospecting should be a part of the overall company strategy whereby sales distribution, production, marketing and finance are all closely interconnected. An imbalance between any of these areas can lead to huge problems in product delivery, which will affect cash flow, customer relations and company development. The company strategy will be a factor in deciding how much of the product needs to be produced and how much needs to be sold.

Prospecting is about looking for and finding new customers. It involves targeting and focusing on an identified group who you think may buy your product. It also means identifying those people who may or may not become your potential customers, that is, qualifying them. Will they be able to afford your product or service? Is it worth investing time and effort in them? Which of your existing or prospective customers represent the best value for the time and effort involved? Prospecting may require some creative thinking about matching product and client: if you are selling sunbeds, your target group could contain people suffering from arthritis as well as those who wish to get a tan. Imaginative prospecting also involves thinking creatively about how your product could be used in ways not initially envisaged. Frisbees were originally designed for young people to play with in a park but gradually were sold more and more in pet stores to provide a fun way for people to exercise their dogs.

Once you decide that a prospect qualifies in terms of ability to purchase, the process moves to a new level, what some authors (for example, Miller and Heiman 1998) describe as the 'sales funnel', or pipeline, or the main selling process. This is an important concept that refers to the need to have a continual moving stream of prospects, so that your company's production cycle is able to match your sales cycle effectively. Consequently, as new prospects come in at one end successful completions are being delivered at the other. Equally, you would decide when a prospect merits qualifying out, that is, the pursuit is not worth the effort.

Prospecting is important for the following reasons.

- Finding new customers is essential for increasing total sales. It is important to keep your sales figures high if you are to maintain credibility with your company and earn a decent income. You need a constant supply of new customers to ensure you are always in business.

- Updates in the manufacturing of your product will mean constantly matching it with new customers' needs; this ensures the growth of your company and yourself, and a regular cash flow. You cannot afford to stand still: you are either growing or shrinking – there is no in-between in organisational development. Prospect feedback is essential to this.

- If you are building up your own business you need to ensure that you have the right customer base. Every penny saved is a penny earned. You cannot afford to waste time and resources inappropriately.

- Customers may have switched to other suppliers for various reasons: those suppliers may have better advertising, or appear to offer a better service. You need to find out what is going on in the field that may have prompted your customer to switch. It is, of course, more cost effective to have retained them in the first place, which emphasises the need for good ongoing customer support.

- Your customer may have needed your product only once, in which case it is your responsibility to keep in touch with them and alert them to any new editions of the product.

- Relationships with some customers may have deteriorated; how do you put the situation right?

- Your existing customers may have moved out of your area, or have gone out of business.

- Normal wastage: existing customers may have outgrown your product, moved house or even died.

You need to have in-depth knowledge of your customer and your product, including its strengths, limitations, advantages, how it operates, service backup, running costs and delivery – all these aspects must be at your fingertips. Benefits are not benefits unless they match the customer's needs so intelligence on their situation is important. You also need to know about what your competitors are up to and how they sell. This enables you to match your product and relate its benefits to your customer's needs. Knowledge of all aspects is essential: if you are selling books you need to know what the books say and how they will benefit the customer. If you are selling fishing rods you need a good working knowledge of the sport in general and where your product fits; it would help if you also enjoy fishing and know the different categories. If you do not have the right level of knowledge you should do some research to develop it. If you are not clear about anything, you need to develop your knowledge so that you will demonstrate your credibility as a salesperson and communicate this appropriately to your customer.

Believe in your product. It does not need to be top of the range in any one area but you must be able to believe in the balance of the cost benefits it delivers to your customer. Most people admire but would not wish to purchase a Rolls Royce; they simply want a good, reliable car they can afford and that will give good fuel consumption. You need to be convinced that your product will give good value to the people who buy it. People buy for their own individual reasons.

Prospecting should become part of your daily routine. A set period of time a day dedicated to prospecting can keep your business on track. The more time you invest in prospecting the more likely you are to achieve and maintain a thriving clientele. Time spent should be productive. At any point in time you should know that what you are doing is moving you closer to your goal. It is easy to be a busy fool or carry out irrelevant tasks to look busy. It is important to have a written plan of activity for the months ahead and a timetable for each day. The written plan should state targets for each area of activity. This keeps focus on the balance of activity between looking for new clients and working with existing ones. Set aside specific hours to prospect and to contact. Doing your action research can help you to do this.

Assess your strengths and limitations honestly in relation to your capacity to selling your product. Do this regularly, especially at various points in the sales process where you feel you are strong. This will almost certainly show you areas where you need to improve what you are doing. If you are not good at prospecting, you need to spend time and energy learning how to do it better. This brings us to the next section, which is about how you can research your practice in the area.

How Do I Research Prospecting in Action?

This section contains ideas about how you can research and evaluate your prospecting practice in action. Here is a generic action plan for how you might do this. A more specific plan appears in the case study that follows.

FORM OF QUESTIONS YOU WOULD USE

At this point you would probably use diagnostic questions about your practice and current situation. Diagnosis should not be taken in its medical sense that something is wrong, more that something needs checking as part of a regular evaluation process. If something is amiss, you need to know what it is so you can plan for improvement. Beware of those who say, 'If it ain't broken, don't fix it.' Ask, 'How can it be improved?' This constant attitude of alertness and openness to change also helps to avoid potential problems in the future.

It also raises the issue of 'improvement'. As a professional you need to strive to improve all the time, to stay on top of your game. Olympic champions practise consistently. If you rest on your laurels you will soon go backward, simply because other people are going forward. The champion golfer Gary Player is reputed to have said, 'The more I practise the luckier I get.' It is the same in any process.

Here is a possible action plan for researching prospecting. In this chapter we set out the questions you would ask in detail. In later chapters we suggest other ways of communicating the process of an action enquiry.

QUESTIONS YOU CAN ASK

What do I need to investigate?

First identify an area you need to investigate. This may involve taking stock of your overall practices of prospecting to identify those areas that are working well and those that need attention. You can do this using a traditional SWOT analysis (strengths, weaknesses, opportunities and threats) or benchmarking system, where you compare your business metrics with those of other similar businesses or industries. Elliott (1991) refers to this stocktaking exercise as a reconnaissance phase. You may find that you are spending too much time reading about rival companies rather than telephoning potential new customers. There may be a number of reasons: you could be putting things off, or simply not aware of what you should be doing. Aim to identify and focus on what you are doing well and what you could do better.

Once you have identified your area of enquiry, formulate a research question of the kind, 'How do I find out what I am doing well? How do I find new ways of prospecting and identifying new customers? How do I improve this aspect?'

Why do I need to investigate this area?

Prospecting is vital to the success of your business. You need a constant stream of new customers to ensure its viability. If you can deliver a good service to these customers, they may in turn recommend you to their contacts, so you will build up a steady stream of returning customers.

Prospecting ensures that you are clear about the value of your product for your potential customers. You may find that you need to re-think whether your product is actually meeting their needs. Although not every contact may end in a sale, it will provide positive useful feedback that will help you to shape your product appropriate to your customers' needs.

Prospecting means living your value of maximum performance in selling. Your stocktake will show whether you are living this value in practice. If you are, how do you show it to others? If you are not, why not? How can you change the situation so that you are?

What is the situation like now?

Gather data to gain objective insights into what you are doing and whether things are as you wish them to be. You could keep daily records of activity and record the amount of time you spend on each activity such as contacts made and the outcomes, and record what you learned. Methods for gathering this kind of data could include keeping logs using record books or computer spreadsheets, personal tape-recorded memos, and reflective journals to record the experience itself and your learning from it. This may also take the form of a video diary. Social media can be useful: you could compare your results with the experiences of other colleagues on Facebook or Twitter.

As part of overall company strategy, prospecting happens usually with the involvement of the sales manager. You may be able to access your company's sales projections and growth figures, based on their requirements to keep production going and add growth to developing the company. You will be able to match your actual sales figures with these projections and identify where there may be a possible mismatch. From a strategic perspective, selling needs to be matched to the ability of the company to produce, deliver and service the product. Too few sales reduce the company's income; too many sales can cause serious cash flow and production problems.

What can I do? What will I do?

Write in your reflective diary all your options for action. Your organisation may provide you with contacts and leads. Aim to do some strategic planning, involving issues such as: Who do you think you can contact? How many do you think you can contact in a day? How much do you think you can reasonably do in a day or a week?

Targeting: You can find groups using electoral rolls, newspapers, telephone books and advertisements. You can visit trade shows, or look at practices in the local environment: young parents dropping their children off at school are not so likely to buy luxury cruises. You can visit conferences: if you are hoping to sell your professional education course or your consultancy services, you will aim for only those groups who work in your field. Some organisations may provide leads or appointments and many salespeople exist on these, but you may also need more to enhance your performance. You may also be self-employed so have no contact with company resources.

When pre-qualifying customers you would study the demographics to make sure you are targeting the appropriate age range, income group or size of company appropriate to your product. Drive around a prospective area and study it to assess whether the people down this street or catchment area are likely to buy your product. See what you can surmise from clues about the demographic. If they appear to be a likely target group you can try certain strategies, including, for example, a letter drop in an identified catchment area where people are likely to buy your product. You could send out an email-shot to people in your target industry with pointers to relative topics on your website.

Try cold calling with discretion: this is generally not considered the best strategy, as potential customers may get angry at your telephoning or turning up at their office out of the blue.

When prospecting, as in all stages of the sales process, remember that you are selling the benefits of your product, not the product itself. Who is likely to need these benefits? If you are selling lawnmowers, few customers are interested in the revolutions per minute and want to know instead that it cuts the grass in less time than other lawnmowers.

A useful strategy to improve prospecting is to draw up an action plan, which you can develop to different levels of sophistication. At a basic level you can write down target numbers per day and tick them off when you have achieved them. This figure is related to how many sales you need to make to keep your business viable. If you need to make 4 sales a week and your close rate is 1 sale in 3 presentations, then you will need on average 12 presentations per week to make 4 sales. Therefore if your average success rate is 1 appointment per 5 telephone calls, you will need to make 60 calls per week. Whichever system you work with, make sure it is right and workable for you.

You could try forming alliances with other businesses so you can refer customers to each other. You could exchange materials such as brochures, and avail of each other's client lists.

You could attend trade shows where you can advertise your product, and look at trade advertisements and identify companies that may benefit from your product. This may mean that you need to collect better data to give you a more detailed picture of who your customer is. In some cases you may need to sell the concept to an end user who then persuades their supplier to purchase from you.

The main principle here is the need to think creatively about what you can achieve and then decide to implement your proposed action plan. Once you come up with your action plan, the next step is to try it out in action. It may work or it may not. If it does, all well and good. If not, you will need to try a different strategy.

How do I check that any conclusions I reach are reasonably fair and accurate?

To check whether you are succeeding in improving your prospecting, you would continue gathering data to show how the situation is unfolding. You would generate evidence from the data (Chapter 7), which can act as the grounds for your claim that you think you have improved your practice. Your evidence will show you whether you are on the right track – what does it show you about your success rate? Remember too that negative experiences can help to guide you closer to more successful ones. You can also do an effort–reward analysis in terms of how much time, money and effort you spend on developing possibilities; this will help you to compare your success rate with other people's and perhaps learn from the way they approach their potential customers.

How do I modify my practice in light of my evaluation?

Acting on the intelligence you have gathered so far, you will develop your new prospects into customers. Increasing the number of customers who are likely to buy your product or services will help you and your organisation to grow. You can proceed with reasonable confidence that your new prospects will become buyers, and generate a greater number of successful sales.

How do I explain the significance of my action research?

You can explain why it is important to develop your prospecting practices through studying what you are doing, matching new figures to old and learning from experience. You have found new more useful directions and are focusing your energies in more productive ways.

The following case study shows the process above in action.

CASE STUDY

My name is Margaret. I live in England and I am building up my own consultancy business in marketing and public relations. I am focusing on how I can attract new customers to make my business viable.

What area do I need to investigate?

I know that large and medium-sized companies operate in this area of business in my locality, aggressively marketing their services. As I do not have any strategic alliances with these companies I have decided that I need to target niche areas, mainly small local businesses and new start-ups. In order to enhance my chances I will also target larger and medium-sized businesses who may be open to my approach. I also need to understand my own business thoroughly, what it offers and what makes it distinctive from others. My first concern therefore is how I can access and attract clients, so I need to check whether my prospecting is effective. In this case my prospecting also becomes a piece of field research into the needs of local companies, which might in turn alter the service I offer.

Why do I need to investigate this area?

I need to investigate this area because, as a newly developing business, my starting point is to identify and connect with potential clients. So I need to research my prospecting to develop an understanding of it, learn how to do it effectively and identify areas that need improvement. Unless I do this I may waste time chasing inappropriate clients.

Also, dealing with new start-ups and small and medium-sized businesses fits my values and ethos, in that I believe in individual entrepreneurialism and a more democratic delivery of business not completely dominated by large business groups.

How do I gather data?

First I need to investigate how I am actually allocating my time to different aspects of this prospecting. I need to keep a daily record of what I do, and record the time spent on each area of the business. I will record contacts made and outcomes. I will allocate specific time to strategy development, planning, researching and contacting. By doing this I can gather baseline data that will show me which areas I need to focus on and strengthen.

What can I do? What will I do?

I will record the results of each area of activity on a daily basis so that I have a working idea of the percentage of success I can initially expect in each of the areas. Did my planning come to fruition? Did my research provide me with useful information? Was my contacting response positive?

How will I check that any conclusions I come to are reasonably fair and accurate?

Having developed a baseline of activity level I will try to reflect on my action on a regular basis in order to assess progress continually. The results of each part of the activity will be measurable in terms of outcomes. I will also ask for feedback from potential clients to indicate their response to my way of connecting with them. I will join forums and talk to others where we can share experience and give feedback. This is also another area for prospecting.

How will I modify my practice in light of my evaluation?

I will observe which areas of my activity seem to be the most effective and jettison activities that seem to bring no return. This is aligned to Pareto's 80/20 principle, where 20 per cent of my activity brings 80 per cent of my results, so I need to identify which is the fruitful 20 per cent.

What is the significance of what I have done in my action research?

Starting from zero I will have developed a database of possible contacts and used different means of communication to connect with possible clients. By doing this I will know what I can deliver because I am best positioned to judge with clients whether we can work together for mutual benefit. I have demonstrated how I have tried to think creatively how to make the best use of varied resources.

Summary

This chapter is about designing and planning your action research study. It introduces ideas about some of the methodologies and values appropriate to action research, and discusses the positioning of the researcher in the enquiry. It emphasises the importance of identifying theoretical frameworks and grounds these in the literatures. Designing an action research study is linked with prospecting as the first stage in the sales process. Prospecting involves finding, qualifying and targeting new prospective customers. The next stage is connecting and appointing, which forms the focus of Chapter 5.

Chapter 5

Strategic Action Planning: Connecting and Appointing

This chapter is about drawing up strategic action plans to guide your action research. You will be able to explain to others, including colleagues in your company and your academic supervisors, what you hope to achieve and how you plan to do so. The connecting and appointing phase of the sales process is used as an example, because this also involves drawing up strategic action plans. You plan how you are going to connect with customers to make an appointment. In the first stage of your sales research, when you focused on prospecting (Chapter 4) you asked, 'Who am I going to sell to?' Now you ask, 'How am I going to do this? How do I connect and meet with prospects so I can sell them the product?'

Action planning for your research involves:

- planning what you are going to do;

- being clear about why you intend to do it, that is, offering a rationale for your actions;

- identifying the procedures for doing research, including choosing participants, attention to ethical issues, and arranging the resources and timeline for your research;

- identifying and considering how to deal with any logistical and practical issues that may help or hinder you.

Action planning for sales success involves:

- knowing the received wisdom about sales;

- evaluating what you are doing well and perhaps not so well;

- identifying what you need to do better.

The chapter covers these sections.

- What are the principles of strategic action planning?

- What are the principles of connecting and appointing?

- How do I research connecting and appointing in action?

What Are the Principles of Strategic Action Planning?

At some point in your research programme you will be required to do a formal project, so here is some advice about what areas to think about. They include the following:

- drawing up action plans in action research;

- monitoring practices and gathering and analysing data.

DRAWING UP ACTION PLANS IN ACTION RESEARCH

Key literatures outline what drawing up action plans in action research involves. McNiff and Whitehead (2010: 112) identify the following areas:

- planning, designing and preparing;

- resourcing;

- working with other people;

- deciding feasibility;

- ensuring ethical behaviour;

- doing your research project;

- evaluating the significance of the research;

- writing up the project;

- disseminating provisional findings;

- articulating its importance.

This is what they involve.

Planning, designing and preparing

- *Identify a research area and issue.* You identify a research area and a specific issue (see Chapter 4). This gives your research a firm anchoring.

- *Initial reading and literature search.* You engage with the literatures on a formal study programme. You are expected to read core research methods texts at any level, and also develop a firm understanding of basic methodological issues. At masters and advanced study level you will study issues of epistemology and philosophy. You also need to study and develop your subject knowledge, in your case, the theory and practices of sales.

- *Draw up an ethics statement.* Early in your research, draw up an ethics statement, letters requesting permission to do your research and letters inviting participants to be involved. You must get authorisation to do your research from appropriate ethics committees at your institution and with your company.

- *Plan and design your project.* Make sure you are confident about methodological issues and how to design and manage a project. If in doubt, ask a colleague in your company and/or your academic advisor.

Resourcing

- *Money.* Your main resources are money, time, other people and facilities. Check with your company if they are willing to fund your studies. If they are, draw up a realistic budget and stick to it; aim to show that their faith in you is justified. Do not expect funding and be prepared to fund yourself if necessary. Study fees are high everywhere so be sure you will be able to complete your studies before you embark on them.

- *Time*. Check whether you will be given release time from work for your studies. This is unlikely, and most mature learners simply make time to do their studies. This usually means putting something out of life (evening TV or weekend sport) in order to put study in. Be aware of what you are letting yourself in for (but so worthwhile when you get the qualification). Also remember to liaise with your friends and family, so they are happy to give you time and space to get on with your studies. This may need some negotiation and everyone's willingness to stick to what is agreed.

- *Reprographics and printing services*. Check whether you may use the company's multimedia and online expertise and facilities where necessary. You may also need to use reprographic services. Higher education institutions still expect printed theses and dissertations.

Working with other people

- *Discuss with management and keep them informed*. Discuss everything with management and policy makers at periodic intervals. They may be glad for you to feed back your research findings to the company so others can learn from your research and be inspired to conduct research themselves. In this way they can develop their company into a learning organisation (Chapter 8).

- *Identify potential research participants*. Also identify and invite potential groups of colleagues and customers to be involved as participants in your research. At a practical level you hope to turn the sales experience into an encounter where all parties learn. At all stages, especially at the consolidating stage (Chapter 7), customers can give you valuable feedback about your performance. If they decide not to go ahead with the sale they will give you feedback about their reasons, and whether this had anything to do with your performance.

- *Identify potential critical friends*. You can invite colleagues and customers to be critical friends to give you feedback on progress and offer ideas about how you could strengthen your research. Some may offer to be in your validation group, where you would present your research to an identified group at periodic intervals (Chapter 7). You could invite customers to be participants in these validation groups: if you are selling to other companies, for example, they may wish to disseminate your findings to their own salesforce. You could invite your academic supervisor too, to lend scholarly authority to the proceedings.

Deciding on the feasibility of your research

- *Achievablity.* Is everything achievable? Will you be able to do your research in the time available? Will you get access to texts? Make sure you can access the online database of your institution's library. How much support does your academic supervisor offer? All institutions have agreed guidelines about this.

- *Power relationships in your company.* Is your topic likely to be vetoed by management or will they welcome the idea of your research and its promise of company professionalisation? Will you encounter the power of other people's possible jealousies?

- *Expectations of organisational cultures.* Think about your organisation's culture and how they will respond to your research. Cultures vary: in boardroom contexts research is often highly valued; in shopfloor contexts it is sometimes considered weird if a salesperson reads a book. This can be tricky if it applies to you, because reading is essential if you want to improve what you are doing and not simply continue doing more of the same. Aim to cultivate an image of courteous, quietly confident and understated professionalism. This helps ensure that you will not encounter hostility and can pursue your chosen goals.

Considering ethics and access

- *Ensuring ethical project management.* This involves securing permission from everyone involved (participants, critical friends, customers and colleagues) to have the data they give you made public, which requires you to contact them and get their permission. Permissions should be in writing. Assure your participants of anonymity, confidentiality if they wish, access to their data, unreserved permission to withdraw from the research and, if so, to have data about them destroyed.

- *Clearing your research plan with institutions and management.* You must get permission from the ethics committee of your accrediting institution, and from your company to proceed with the research. You may not proceed without this permission.

- *Keeping your word.* You must keep your word. If you do not people will not trust you anymore. You could also face litigation because you could in some cases be acting outside the law.

Doing your research project

Check that you are reasonably familiar with all these action steps:

- identify research issue and question;

- articulate research question(s);

- gather baseline data;

- identify working criteria and standards of judgement;

- imagine solutions: brainstorm with colleagues;

- gather data on an ongoing basis;

- generate evidence from the data;

- articulate knowledge claim and test its validity through specific validation procedures;

- convene validation group;

- explain possible modification of thinking and practice;

- articulate the significance of the project and your findings.

In relation to connecting and appointing these steps involve aspects listed below. This kind of action plan can act as a roadmap when doing your project.

- *Identify an area of interest.* Your area of interest may be something you are troubled, curious or intrigued about. Example: 'My appointments diary is not very full. What is going on?'

- *Specify a research issue and question.* Articulate a research question. Example: 'How do I connect more effectively and get more appointments?' or 'How do I learn to qualify prospects more effectively?' Remember the question may change as you work through your enquiry – for example: 'I need to create more time to service all my client accounts. How do I do this?'

- *Outline the aims of your research.* Keep your immediate aims manageable and achievable, within a longer-term aim. Example: 'My aim is to discover why I am not getting appointments. I would like to find ways of turning this around so that I am getting lots of them. In the longer term I will have so many accounts that I will need my own sales team.'

- *Explain the reasons and purposes of the research.* Keep the reasons practical and relate them to your values. Example: 'My income is suffering because I am not getting the appointments I need. I must get more appointments in order to sell more. I want to realise my values of business excellence and company profitability.' (You will use these values as criteria and standards as a way of judging the success of your research – see below.)

- *Gather initial data to show what the situation is like at the beginning of the enquiry and throughout.* Data gathering is a core part of research and involves choosing from a range of methods. At the beginning of your research you gather baseline data to show the current situation. Example: 'My diary in August 2014 shows an average of only four confirmed qualified appointments per week.' You continue to gather data throughout your research to show how the situation progresses (hopefully improves). Example: 'My diary in October 2014 shows that I am averaging nine confirmed qualified appointments per week.')

- *Identify success criteria and standards to help you make judgements about progress, and quality of work and practice.* You can identify criteria and standards of judgement in relation to your values – for example, profitability, customer satisfaction, business excellence and sustainable progress. Example: 'A main criterion for judging quality in my practice is whether I can show that I am getting more appointments. The fact that my customers agree to meet with me indicates I am doing something right.'

- *Generate evidence in relation to those criteria to show progress or lack of it.* Use these criteria to select data from your data archive that will stand as evidence to show their realisation in practice. Example: 'Does my data archive contain pieces that show the criteria in action? Can I find instances of connecting with customers and making appointments?'

- *Come to provisional conclusions about the success of your research so far.* Consider whether your criteria have been achieved so you can make judgements about the success of your practice and research. Example: 'I can show that I am demonstrating professional practices because my appointments book is getting full. Customers have emailed to say they enjoyed speaking with me on the phone and are looking forward to our appointment.'

- *Test the validity of these provisional conclusions.* Test the validity of your conclusions against the critical feedback of peers, customers and appropriate others. Example: 'I can check with customers whether I am right in thinking they found our telephone conversation interesting, informative and useful.'

- *Draw warranted conclusions.* From your findings you begin to draw conclusions. These always need to be grounded in the evidence and tested against identified criteria. Example: 'I believe I am justified in thinking that I have established a good relationship with my customer. I can produce email and mobile text evidence to show this. Also my customer has responded to my blog, so other people can see this too.'

- *Change thinking and practice in light of these conclusions.* From your learning, change direction in your thinking and practice as appropriate. Your evidence shows that Internet methods work better than paper mailshots. You might consider developing a personal website linked with the company one. Example: 'My customer is telling everyone on Twitter about our informative and useful first contact conversation. They are a big company and are tweeting all their subsidiaries.'

Evaluate the significance of the research

Aim to produce working documents about the significance of your project for others' learning and for your own. You can influence organisational learning and behaviours through doing so. Example: 'I am writing a report for a company presentation on how I have managed to increase the number of appointments through studying and improving how I make email contact with potential customers.'

Writing up the project

Write your draft report and send to work-based colleagues and academic supervisor for approval and modification. Chapter 9 outlines how to write a report.

Disseminating provisional findings

Think about how to disseminate your findings through conferences, books and journal articles, appearances on local radio and television, convening special interest groups, liaising with others through social networking. You can influence other people's thinking and practices through blogs, websites and articles. Example: 'I will post my diary online and invite customers to contact me. I will ask customer X if I can make a videotape of our conversation and post it on YouTube.'

Articulating its importance

It is important to appreciate the significance of your research, and to be able to communicate this to different individuals and groups, such as your manager, customers and organisation. The significance of your research would include ideas about how you have generated your own theory of professional practice through studying your practice, and how you can influence others to do the same. By articulating the significance of your research you are able to show how you have re-identified yourself as a researcher, and are now speaking with your researcher's voice.

MONITORING PRACTICES AND GATHERING AND ANALYSING DATA

Data is central to your research project because it is where all the information about the planning, process and outcomes is stored. There are dozens of books on data and data gathering. Here are some main issues.

When gathering data think about these things:

- what data to look for;

- how to gather it;

- how to analyse and interpret it;

- how to monitor practices over time (this issue is dealt with in Chapter 7).

What data to look for

You are looking for data that show how you are achieving your aims over time. Because your aims reflect the values that inform your practices, you are looking for data that show your values in action: if dialogue is a main value you will look for those actions that show you and your customer in dialogue. In action research there is an assumption that learning informs action; and that one person's actions inform another person's thinking and learning, and consequently their actions. You can understand this as:

- my learning informs my actions;

- my actions inform my customer's learning;

- my customer's learning informs their actions;

- my customer's actions inform my learning.

This becomes a cyclical process of mutually influencing processes of learning and actions. You learn and act together. You can find this idea fully developed in McNiff (2013a).

How to gather it

You look for data in all the interactions of your project, in all possible forms. Data are those pieces of information you gather using different methods. There are different types of data including:

- quantitative statistical data (how many or how much of something);

- qualitative data (how meaningful it was).

You can use a range of methods for gathering these different types of data. The most commonly used methods for gathering statistical data are:

- experiments;

- observations and recordings;

- obtaining data from information systems;

- closed-question questionnaires and structured surveys (online, postal, or face-to-face).

To gather qualitative data you could use:

- unstructured and open-ended questionnaires and surveys;

- interviews and focus groups;

- audio and video recordings;

- social networking, blogs and websites;

- narrative accounts;

- diaries and journals;

- drawings, graphic diaries, charts and mapping devices;

- portfolios … and so on.

Many good books offer advice about these methods: for example, Creswell (2007); Cohen et al. (2011); Mason (2010); Yin (2009): see also McNiff and Whitehead (2010, 2011) for more detailed ideas about data and evidence.

Once you have gathered all your data keep it in a data archive. This could be in a filing cabinet, on your computer, in a drawer, or wherever is convenient and appropriate to your work. Your data archive is dynamic and live: aim to sort your data on a regular basis. First you sort it into categories, such as 'prospects contacted' or 'emails from prospects'; you then begin to differentiate these categories into sub-categories such as 'prospects in news agencies; prospects in public houses'; or 'emails from the company' and 'emails about key accounts'.

Aim to gather data at each and every phase of the sales process: in prospecting you maintain lists of potential customers; in connecting and appointing you keep records of your appointments, information you have sent to prospects and details of arrangements; in presenting you keep records of who said what and what agreements were reached; and in consolidating and developing you keep records of goods dispatched and customer satisfaction rates. Be as imaginative as you wish when gathering and sorting data. The main thing is to gather it, and keep it all until the research is completed (and after this too, because it may be relevant for future research, though you would have to ask participants' permission to use it again).

How to analyse and interpret it

As part of the data-gathering process, aim to establish criteria for judging its quality. A criterion is a sign by which we judge quality: when you book a hotel room you anticipate that the hotel will be warm, comfortable and clean. Warmth, comfort and cleanliness become criteria (to note, 'criterion' is singular; 'criteria' is plural). The same principle applies in sales: if you are hoping for customer satisfaction, then customer satisfaction becomes a criterion, as do efficiency, punctuality, good conduct, professional behaviour and a thousand other qualities. These qualities link strongly with your values: your values become your criteria and the standards by which you judge quality, as they emerge in practice. However, although this is a core methodological point, in practice it can be tricky because different people have different values, so you need to negotiate your values with those of the other people in the encounter, including your customer and colleagues.

Look through your data archive with your values-as-criteria in mind, and identify those pieces of data that show the criteria in action. You can show, for example, an email from a customer thanking you for prompt delivery of the goods (prompt delivery is a value that acts as a criterion); or a videotape of you and a colleague practising interviewing techniques through role play (careful listening is a value that acts as a criterion); or a memo from your company manager congratulating you on the number of sales – or even your 'salesperson of the month' photograph hanging on the office wall (excellent sales results is a value that acts as a criterion). These data will act potentially as evidence (see Chapter 7, which is about evaluating).

We now look at the relevance of these ideas to the practices of connecting and appointing.

What Are the Principles of Connecting and Appointing?

First think about the aims and outcomes of connecting and appointing.

AIMS OF CONNECTING AND APPOINTING

The aims of connecting and appointing are to make contact with prospective customers, qualify them and, if they qualify, arrange to meet with them. You aim to get their attention, engage their interest and create a desire that will lead to the action of making an appointment or arranging a meeting. The aim at this point is not to sell the product, just to arrange a meeting.

ANTICIPATED OUTCOMES

You anticipate that your prospective customer will agree to meet with you. You will then have an opportunity to sell them your product.

Here are the main principles of connecting and appointing.

THE PRINCIPLES OF CONNECTING AND APPOINTING

Having used the prospecting process to identify suitable candidates (Chapter 4) the next step is to establish contact with a view to arranging a meeting where you can make a presentation and hopefully sell your product. Initial contact may be conducted online by a prospect you have directed to your website. This could be via email, Skype or a similar system until the prospect feels ready for a personal meeting as their confidence in your professionalism grows.

It is important not to try to sell the product at this stage so much as to sell the idea of meeting in order to discuss possibilities. Trying to sell the product too early in the process can often frighten and alienate the client. As you have not yet presented to the customer you cannot yet fully understand their needs and wants.

Many prospects nowadays want to investigate a product thoroughly online before agreeing to a face-to-face meeting. This allows the safety of collecting intelligence without the likely pressure of personal contact with a salesperson. They may even have looked up your personal profiles. This underlines the importance of a well-presented, informative and customer-friendly online presence as part of the sales process.

Now, having gained the client's attention, it is important that you know what to do with it. You can cater on having their attention only for a short time, so you need to develop their interest. Use your judgement to find the right balance between quickly outlining the benefits that this client will gain and not coming on so powerfully as to frighten and alienate them. It may be appropriate briefly to state the overall benefit of the product to your customer and indicate who else has purchased it and how they have benefited, in order to capture their interest. If not, focus only on making the appointment.

Connecting and appointing is a first opportunity for you to establish your credibility so that your prospective client will agree to meet you. Most customers want to know, 'What is in it for me?' and at this stage they will probably ask themselves, 'Is this a good use of my time?' Aim to present yourself as a knowledgeable and pleasant professional who knows what they are talking about, including good quality market information. Be able to summarise the unique selling points that set you apart. By focusing on making your product benefits explicit, which is what the prospect wants to hear about, you will automatically communicate the quality of your professionalism. Never talk down (or up) to your customer, and avoid patronising at all costs. Show that you respect your customer as an intelligent consumer who is aware that they have choices.

Make sure the person you are dealing with is a decision maker or a person who can influence the decision maker to buy. Often the potential user of the product is not the budget holder; this is especially the case in large organisations. To reach a purchase decision you would usually need to have the support of both these people.

Even if the customer's decision is not to meet at this point but possibly in the future, agree when this might be and who will do what in the meantime. It is always a good idea to set mutually agreed targets throughout developmental processes.

Key strategies for successful connecting and appointing are indicated below. Many of them are linked with the literatures of psychology and philosophy.

FIT FOR LEARNING

My name is Frank. I have been selling hygiene products business to business into the manufacturing sector for over 20 years and had built up a steady pattern of constant selling to people I knew. Then came the economic downturn in 2008 and my world changed quickly. People I had known well for years disappeared, some bought out by new kinds of people who had little time and money to invest with me. I considered giving up sales and looked for alternative employment.

During this time I took an online course in philosophy and stumbled across action research. I decided to test out the ideas in my existing situation. This fresh look gave me insights into how I had settled into a comfortable non-challenging routine and was psychologically unfit for learning. My most difficult hurdle was to unlearn the habits that had worked well and realise that I was in fact a middle-aged rookie. Accepting this unleashed a desire to learn about this new world from the ground up. As I still had a large existing database and connections in the industry, the first issue to investigate was how I made contact with the new breed of prospect that had replaced the old. I sent a small number of personalised emails to selected prospects. I introduced myself and my company and passed on useful industry links and information. I then followed up with further emails saying I would be keen to meet at a time convenient to the customer to tell them more about the service we provided widely across the industry. I realised that the 'killer letter' (the one that always leads to a 'yes') does not exist and that I had to make many more initial contacts before succeeding in getting an appointment. In fact I realised I was providing an information service to prospects before I actually got to meet them. This, however, paid dividends when we finally met.

How Do I Research Connecting and Appointing in Action?

This section contains ideas about how to research your practice in action, using the critical questions outlined on pages 42–3. You are investigating how you can evaluate and where necessary improve your practices of appointing and connecting.

FORM OF QUESTIONS ASKED

At this point you ask strategic questions. This enables you to focus on key issues prior to taking action, including how you are going to connect and get appointments with people. In many cases it becomes a process of selecting options: who is your key account and which customer group will you contact? Who is most likely to generate most value for money and time invested? If you are a hotel manager, will you give special offers to irregular customers who bring in variable income or will you target and connect with regular corporate executives and agencies?

You also focus on clarifying what your overall aims are in connecting; this influences how you will act towards your customer and what you will do to gain competitive edge – that is, what you will do and offer that leads people to connect with you rather than your competitors. This requires in-depth knowledge of your competitors, their products and methods. It also involves a thorough stocktake of what you do well and what you could do better, especially with regard to honing your skills about how to connect and get the appointments you want.

Here is a generic action plan of how you might do this. A more specific plan is outlined in the case study that follows.

How do I improve my practices in connecting and appointing?

You have identified people who may be suitable candidates for a sale, so your next step is to connect with them in a way most appropriate and acceptable for your product.

However, you may feel that your connecting and appointing practice is not going as well as it should be. Initial approaches are not turning into invitations to arrange a meeting. This could be disastrous for you as you will not be able to make the presentations on which your customer's ultimate agreement to purchase depends. You need to find where the slippage lies: this could be between the initial information you send out and when you make your first telephone call or send an email; or between this telephone call or email and an agreement to arrange a meeting.

Why do I wish to investigate this area?

You need to meet with and make a presentation to decision makers in their homes or in the setting of the industry you are targeting. They will often be busy people with demands on their time, so it is important they feel confident that a meeting with you will be in their interests. Aim therefore to meet with them as individuals whenever possible, which means making direct contact and introducing yourself. An initial introduction is essential as you are not as likely to get a favourable response if you call cold.

From your perspective, failure to connect would carry serious consequences, because it would mean a reduced number of presentations and therefore a lower number of sales. It would mean also that you were not selling the product you are committed to, so it could mean not achieving personal satisfaction in selling.

How will I gather data to show the situation as it is?

Aim to gather data on a systematic basis to give you a supply of important and necessary information. For example, keep a record of decision makers in the area of the companies and industries you are targeting. Find out who they are by consulting their directories and websites. Build up a central file containing the names and contact information for the individuals you wish to meet.

Also aim to meet with people with influence within businesses, such as the foreman of a machine tool shop. Check whether they are the end user of the product you are selling or the budget holder, and remember that to sell your product you will need to meet with the decision maker, whichever role they occupy, in the setting where your product will be used.

What can I do? What will I do?

Decide how you are going to make contact: there are many ways of doing this. You could do any or all of the following:

- Put on a training day about an aspect of the product you are selling that potential customers would find interesting and useful. Send out invitations to any individuals or groups you are targeting and explain that there is something in it for them.

- Use online methods to send information about your product directly to potential purchasers with key questions for them to begin a dialogue. Decide which information to send and include a link to your website.

- Send brochures to targeted individuals or groups with a covering letter explaining who you are and saying that you will follow up this initial letter with a personal call or visit. Explain what your product is, and give the potential customer some ideas of its benefits so they will know who you are when you call. Do all this in a sincere way and avoid alienating people through over-familiarity or 'false bonhomie'. Make sure you keep a record of all contacts, on your computer, index cards, mobile phone or notepad.

- If you try telephone list approaches, keep lists of contacts and keep them up to date.

- Wherever possible, send some information and introductory literatures by post or email to the client and indicate that you will be following up with a personal contact by telephone or email. Direct prospects to your website highlighting areas of special potential interest.

- When you connect with them, immediately begin to establish the credibility of yourself and your organisation. Make some brief statements about the history of your company and about the general situation in the industry relating to the client's work context. This shows you are up to date with any contexts relating to their situation and can understand any dilemmas. It also demonstrates that you have experience in the area and you know what you are talking about. Do not get into a detailed discussion about costs, logistics or practicalities. These aspects will be covered in the meeting you are calling to arrange.

- Be prepared for this contact. Do some background reading about your prospective customer. Look at their website and profiles on social networking media so you are familiar with their background and current context. Read their literature. Also do your homework about your competitors. Get to know what they are doing and the special features of their products. Check if they are making any special offers that you may need to form a response to.

- Put this information on your notepad so you can refer to it in conversation; aim to show your client how your product will meet their business needs. If you are selling to an offshore customer, make sure you are familiar with the customs of the country or region they work in. Ask colleagues who have visited the country and research the area online. Observing indigenous customs is essential for good business practices.

- Prepare what you are going to say in advance and have appropriate information and your diary to hand. Do not feel you have to write out a script, but have some bullet points on your notepad about your client and about what you are going to say. Craft an opening, learn it by heart and modify it as appropriate to the context. Aim to get your message across in a succinct and engaging manner. Do not talk non-stop; aim to turn this into a personalised conversation. Remember the aim is to arouse and sustain your client's interest so they will wish to meet with you and hear more.

- Practise! Rehearse what you are going to say in advance and practise it. Recruit a family member or colleague to listen to you and give you feedback. There is no substitute for advance preparation and dedicated practice.

- If appropriate, quickly link the benefits of your product to your introductory remarks so the client can see how they may benefit. For example, a recent government decision may have affected costs in a certain area; you can explain how using your computerised delivery system would reduce the customer's transportation costs by 20 per cent or £20,000 – it is always a good idea to state a specific figure, which again shows your appreciation of topical issues.

- Be careful not to alienate the client by being over-enthusiastic or over-familiar. Inconsequential chattiness can quickly lose the interest you have worked so hard to establish. Respect the client's time, and remember the customer is interested in finding answers to their question, 'What's in it for me? Why should I give another 30 seconds to this person when I have so much else to do?' Aim to maintain the initiative and drive the conversation forward whilst not being controlling or directive.

- Keep the conversation dynamic and action-oriented. The underlying message should always be, 'We can help you. Can we get together to discuss how best to do this?'

- When speaking, aim to use the client's name at least twice during the conversation. Using a person's name is a powerful symbol of recognition and regard that can have lasting impact (as can getting the person's name wrong – so do your market research beforehand).

- When your client agrees to meet with you, negotiate a meeting time. If they are flexible, offer two options so they can choose the most convenient. Giving more than two options may simply lead to indecision and promises to get back to you. Say, 'Tuesday morning at 10.15 or Thursday at 2.45 – which of these may be best for you?' Then, having got the appointment, re-confirm the time and date and wish them a good day.

- When you have agreed the appointment, send a follow-up note through the post or by email, to confirm the time and place. This is a demonstration of good personal and business etiquette and also confirms for the client that you are a person to be trusted to act in a professional manner and to deliver the goods.

- You may find you are connected with a personal assistant or administrator. If so, engage with them as you would your prospective client. They will in turn sell you to your client. It does not matter who you are speaking with – everyone deserves respect and courteous behaviour.

- At all times at this stage, remember to sell the appointment, not the product.

How do I evaluate my practice so far? How do I show I am on the right track?

Continue to gather data so you can generate evidence at a later stage to show that you are on the right track. You could keep records to show the ease or difficulty with which you make direct speaking contact with decision makers; this would be a good indicator of effectiveness of your methods. If you are brushed off repeatedly it would be a strong indicator that you have not succeeded in getting your contact's interest so you would need to go back and check whether you have personalised the benefits in a credible way. This kind of data is called disconfirming data, that is, data that show you that things are not working as you hope they would. It can provide valuable feedback that can act as a steer towards corrective action.

Another kind of data would be if your prospective client were to initiate the first conversation: this would be a strong indicator to show that you have aroused their interest. Made and broken appointments could be indicators of the kind of pressure that the client is under, but it could also indicate where you are in their hierarchies of importance. One broken appointment would be understandable; two may be happenstance; three would communicate strongly that your practice was inappropriate in some way, and give you strong feedback that you need to take immediate action to find out what is wrong and improve it. Wherever possible seek feedback from customers, ex-customers and non-customers about how they do or do not want to be contacted. Repeatedly calling a customer at their busiest time of day puts you, your product and company in the box marked 'annoying'.

How will I modify my practices in light of my evaluation?

Effective evaluation depends on maintaining records of activity and records of learning from the experience of those activities. You can, for example, compare the number of conversations initiated with the success rate in terms of appointments made; this gives you useful feedback about which approaches seem most effective. While each industry has its own ways of doing business, it seems that those who think innovatively and are prepared to take risks make the greatest strides forward. This is where inter-organisational thinking and inter-professional learning may be valuable: learning from one industry or group may transfer into another. Awareness of sensitivities is important and avoidance of brashness crucial.

What is the significance of what I have done in my action research?

My action research helps to show that salespeople can develop new strategies by studying their own practice and imagining new solutions to identified issues. By sharing their accounts of practice they can help the sales organisation to adapt to new circumstances and grow.

CASE STUDY

My name is Joseph and I supply a computer programme that matches stock to projected deliveries. I have used my prospecting knowledge to build up a list of clients to contact.

What area do I need to investigate?

I seem to have to make a large number of contacts before I manage to convert these into appointments. My prospecting research has indicated that these are good prospects who would benefit from my product and who would be in a good position to purchase it. There is no common factor that I can identify in the rejections. Quite often the rejections are phrased as postponing a meeting while not refusing to meet. I need to find out why this is happening.

Why do I need to investigate this area?

I need to investigate this area because my connecting and appointing seems to be a weak link in the chain and I am wasting a lot of prospects by failing to convert them. I feel I am not realising the potential of my product, or myself. This is an inefficient part of my sales cycle because I am confident that when I am in front of people I can convince them of the benefits they will receive from purchasing my product. So this area needs urgent attention.

How do I gather data?

I keep good records and breakdown of my activities. I keep records of all the prospects I identify, the results of connecting with them, and the outcomes of presentations. My conversion rate from presentations is reasonably good (2 presentations to 1 sale). My conversion rate from prospects to appointments is poor (20 prospects averaging 2 appointments). This immediately confirms my concerns in this area.

What can I do? What will I do?

I can break down the connecting and appointing into constituent parts and see where the blockage comes in the pipeline. I can note the number of introductory letters and brochures I send and match them with my follow-up telephone calls. I can record my success at getting through to the decision makers so that I will be able to see what the outcome is. I can then compare this with the number of times the decision makers agreed to an appointment. I can try to find a correlation between how many times I made contact and how many times this resulted in an appointment. I can ask for feedback from successful encounters and from people who have found a reason to cancel appointments but were prepared to give feedback.

How will I check that any conclusions I come to are reasonably fair and accurate?

If I spot obvious discrepancies in successful outcomes at any stage this will indicate that I have identified an area that needs remedial action. For example, my initial contacts with decision makers seem friendly and positive but on attempting to make an appointment I find they become more evasive and vague. This indicates the area where the problem lies.

How will I modify my ideas and practice in light of the evaluation?

Using this example I could for instance put a paragraph in my introductory letter saying that I will be ringing in the next few days and would the decision maker kindly mention this to their personal assistant if they feel it is something they would like to hear more about. This helps get past the common problem of a personal assistant protecting their boss from timewasters but inadvertently preventing them from hearing something that would be to the company's advantage. I could also check my communication skills to make sure I am communicating effectively.

What is the significance of what I have done in my action research?

The significance is that I have constructively used my record keeping to provide quantitative and qualitative data about the outcomes of each stage of the connecting and appointing process. I have then tried to come up with some simple approaches to correct discrepancies. My continued record keeping will indicate the outcomes of these changes.

Summary

This chapter is about strategic action planning, which involves visualising how to conduct an action enquiry in order to achieve an identified goal. Action planning is an essential piece of research because it means identifying logistical aspects such as resourcing and time management, and finding ways to take action in order to realise identified values in practice. Strategic action planning is linked with connecting and appointing in sales as the second phase in the sales process. This is where the salesperson gathers intelligence about the prospect in their setting, addressing the issues that could impact on the customer's decision making. This is done for the purpose of making effective contact with the prospect, leading to a sales presentation. Presenting is dealt with in Chapter 6.

Chapter 6

Taking Action and Presenting

This chapter is about implementing your action plans to find ways of achieving your aims and realising your values. In Chapter 5 we considered various options for action. Now it is time to try them out. The presenting phase of the sales process is taken as parallel to the 'taking action' phase of action research. Presenting is the point where you come face to face with your prospective customer, possibly for the first time. The purpose of the meeting is to explore the customer's needs, match those to your company's products, and get a decision to purchase or to move forward in a meaningful way.

The chapter is organised as follows:

- What does taking action in action research involve?

- What are the principles of presenting?

- How do I research presenting in action?

What Does Taking Action in Action Research Involve?

Taking action is a serious business. There are different views in the action research and sales literatures about what it means, and different people adopt different approaches. Here are some of them.

APPROACHES IN THE ACTION RESEARCH LITERATURES

Some action research literatures recommend the following approaches.

A problem-solving approach (akin to a solutions-based approach)

This approach sees action research as problem solving. Johnson (2002: 22) describes the process as follows:

- define the problem;

- generate as many solutions as possible;

- choose a solution that seems the best;

- elaborate and refine;

- implement the solution;

- review, evaluate, and refine as necessary.

This approach, like others, works from the assumptions that (1) the situation you are in presents a problem and (2) there is a solution to the problem. Neither is necessarily the case. Action research is about more than problem solving. It is about improving practices and generating theory from studying interesting and often complex situations, which may deny the idea of 'solution' and instead go with 'best option'.

An interventionist approach

This approach sees action research as a strategy used by a researcher to intervene in their own or someone else's practice (Eikeland 2012). However, intervention may not always be appropriate. While it may be justified on commonsense or humanitarian grounds, as when you stop a child from running into the road, it can also be seen as interference, as, for example, when someone says, 'If I were you I would do it another way.'

A change-management approach

This approach sees action research as a strategy for implementing and managing change (see Parkin 2010, Chapter 2), as when an external person manages other people in an organisation. This is the kind of concept that underpins the language of 'turning organisations (often failing) around'.

APPROACHES IN SALES

The same kinds of approaches have come and gone in sales, such as solutions-based selling (for example, Bosworth 1995).[1] Some contemporary literatures (for example, Johnston and Marshall 2013) take a critical perspective, as we do in this book. These include:

- Salespeople need to check their own motivations. Do they see themselves as 'knower' and the client as 'learner'? Is it their job to persuade the client to make the 'right' decision (that is, to buy what the seller is offering)?

- Customers these days are well educated through accessing information systems, reviewing products online and receiving instant reviews from friends and colleagues via social networking (Chapter 1). Many companies, particularly those with corporate clients, involve customers in product design, construction and production.

- Less charitable reasons, about potential social alienation. Jenkins (1997) describes purchasing from IKEA: customers take large flat-packs of furniture home and put it together, so they need 'to be adept in road haulage and furniture assembly in order to make the concept work' (p. 10). It is common practice that sellers require buyers to print receipts for themselves. Many companies send bills online, or charge customers for paper bills. These impersonal 'them and us' practices are evident across the professions: in healthcare, patients become positioned as objects in receipt of a procedure; in education, as in business, students become customers who receive information. All are 'done to' by an expert. Experts exercise agency; service users don't. In relation to action research, these approaches distort its original conceptualisation as a process where people work together collaboratively for social good. In sales it amounts to competitive arm-wrestling but with no winners.

A collaborative dialogical approach is needed, in research and sales, to combat alienation and encourage personal and social wellbeing. This requires critical mental models about the following:

---

1   See also the critique by the *Harvard Business Review* at http://hbr.org/2012/07/the-end-of-solution-sales/: online, accessed 25 October 2013.

- interrogating motivations in social action and different forms of learning;

- a view of action and reflection as integrated;

- a critical appreciation of what 'change' means;

- a view of self as agent;

- a critical understanding of dialogical processes.

Interrogating motivations in social action and different forms of learning

Taking action means first being aware of our motivations, and whose interests are being served in customer relationships. Recall Habermas's (1972) ideas about technical, practical and emancipatory interests. These, he says, are evolutionary, proceeding from basic to higher order needs, like Maslow's (1954, 1968) hierarchy that works from basic physiological needs for survival to higher order spiritual needs for self-actualisation. Do we espouse technical interests by trying to control a relationship? Or emancipatory interests by interrogating underpinning assumptions and trying to establish intersubjective dialogue?

Think also of Argyris's and Schön's (1978) idea of single loop, double loop and triple loop learning (Chapters 2 and 8). What kind do you aim for in business relationships? Do you aim for single loop learning about subject matters (for example, you and your customer learn about the product)? Or double loop learning where you interrogate your underlying assumptions? Or triple loop learning, where you both evaluate your motivations? Decisions about these matters are not just airy-fairy self-actualisations. Continuous suppression of one's personal values to meet targets can lead to disastrous outcomes such as burnout and alienation.

A view of action and reflection as integrated

Meaningful social action involves reflection on action in action (Schön 1983). We think, 'Is this working? If not, I need to find a different way of doing it.' This can lead to new ways of thinking and working. It is an emancipatory view of action because we can change learned habits and routines in light of better understandings. Schön also talks about ladders of reflection, where we achieve higher levels of reflection by standing back from the situation, allowing more space for re-thinking.

Similarly, Kahneman (2011) talks of System 1 and System 2 thinking. System 1 is a rapid in-the-situation response where we automatically search our memories for similar situations to the one we are in, and look for immediate connections, often by association. If you see a very tall man at an airport and someone asks you, 'Is that man a banker or basketball player?' you are probably more likely to say 'basketball player', given the association of tall men with basketball. A more considered response (System 2 in Kahneman's typology) will encourage you to reflect on the relative numbers of bankers and basketball players and perhaps conclude that, statistically, he is more likely to be a banker.

Achieving this kind of questioning attitude to our own thinking means being open to the idea of change, which can be difficult and requires a conscious decision.

A critical appreciation of what 'change' means

The word 'change' can be used transitively (I change something) and intransitively (I change): you can change your appearance or your clothes. You can also change: the very skin on your body changes by the moment. The world is in a process of change by its nature.

So how do you learn and change your thinking? By listening to and believing what is said, or by critical thinking and transformative learning (Brookfield 1987, 2013; Mezirow 2009), where you transform your thinking through thinking about it? Thinking itself becomes transformative action.

This has implications for your personal and professional dealings. How do you see others? Are they objects you wish to change (or perhaps control)? Whose interests are being served? Acting for social change means acknowledging that change begins in the individual mind: we change our own thinking in order to influence other people to change theirs. We try to influence them to re-think established routines and culturally acquired habits of mind. Many people speak about 'our culture' when defending their right to act in certain ways, forgetting that they make the culture. Remember the GPS TomTom advertisement that says, 'You are not stuck in traffic: you are traffic.'

A view of self as agent

Social action prioritises the need for critical reflection. Difficulties, including wars, begin in local conversations. Packer (2007) describes how the war in Iraq began in an office in the White House. He cites Richard Perle as commenting:

If Bush had staffed his administration with a group of people selected from Brent Scowcroft and Jim Baker, which might well have happened, then it could have been different, because they would not have carried into it the ideas that the people who wound up in important positions brought to it. The ideas are only important as they reside in the minds of people who were involved directly in the decision process (p. 41).

You have the power to change situations, but indirectly, through encouraging others to change themselves. You do this not coercively but through exercising your educational influence. Certainly many people do try to influence in a manipulative way. Foucault (1980) critiqued this practice throughout his lifework, showing how we learn to internalise messages from the culture and apply them without realising it. We end up supervising ourselves and come to believe that these are our own ideas. Chomsky (2005) speaks about the ease of controlling the public mind in totalitarian societies: you force people into compliance and kill them if they resist. Democratic societies, however, have to find other means to do this, so they put in place sophisticated propaganda systems to persuade people to obey; they purchase the media in order to control the culture.

You can take action for positive change, starting with yourself. As a salesperson you should not abuse your power of influence. As a salesperson on a professional education course, it is your responsibility to engage with ideas about ontological, epistemological and political commitments and decide which ones are right for you, and, if not, what other ideas you can put in place.

All these issues depend on the central idea of dialogue and its conditions.

A critical understanding of dialogical processes

Philosophers such as Bohm, Buber and Macmurray developed strong theorisations about what dialogue involves: openness to the other and a readiness before words are spoken to listen and learn. Dialogue is not a case of two monologues that talk past each other. It is a case of active listening and responding to what you hear, not what you wish to hear.

There is another side to dialogue, not well researched in the literatures, which refers to the conditions of dialogue. Being prepared for dialogue means suspending preconceptions, which can be difficult. For those who can do it, fine. For those who cannot, a valuable strategy is to re-frame the question (Schön 1983; Schön and Rein 1994). This again means critique: you look below the question to see the sub-texts, especially those that relate to historical, social and cultural traditions. What brings a person to say they are not worthwhile or that they cannot learn? Look to the hidden influences of the past, to their childhood and historical–cultural experiences. This applies to you too. Are you prejudiced against certain groups or customers? Engaging in genuine dialogue requires us all to think about how we have learned to perceive and position others and ourselves. This awareness can also help us to achieve more sales to people we may have previously disregarded as potential customers.

So, with these matters in mind, now let's turn to the principles of presenting.

What Are the Principles of Presenting?

The aims and anticipated outcomes of presenting are as follows:

AIMS OF PRESENTING

The aim of presenting is to ensure a good customer experience so that the customer is willing to take action, that is, to purchase your product. You do this through adopting a specific methodology of exploring your customer's needs, matching them with your product and getting a decision from your customer to purchase. Ensuring a good customer experience involves certain attitudes and practices from you.

ANTICIPATED OUTCOMES

You anticipate that your customer is going to buy your product, in which case they and you will have achieved your separate and joint aims: they have a product they want and will enjoy, and you have a sale, and the possibility of a returning customer and new referrals.

The sales literatures probably have more advice about presenting than about any other aspect of the sales process. The advice below is drawn from those literatures, from our own experience and from innumerable conversations by us authors with salespeople, customers and business and sales managers around the world. It is all good advice, grounded in many people's many years of experience.

Here are the most common pieces of advice about presenting. They are organised into three broad sections (though there is some overlap between the sections):

1.   characteristics of the sales process;

2.   relating to your customer;

3.   the methodology of presenting.

CHARACTERISTICS OF THE SALES PROCESS

Presenting is at the heart of the sales process. Your job is to ensure a good customer experience while encouraging them to purchase your product. This is the arena where your skills of selling are put to the test and a sale can be achieved or lost. Selling perhaps involves the salesperson's personality more than any other profession and can present considerable demands on your psychological and emotional resources. There is no place to hide in the encounter: you either sell or you don't. It is up to you.

A successful sale usually requires intensive preparation. It is not enough simply to turn up at an appointment. You have to be prepared, and this means doing your background research, about your customer, your product and your competitors.

Presenting is an investigative, research activity. It is vital to have an understanding of your client regarding their need for your product and their overall state of mind, especially whether they are ready to buy. However, the meeting should not take the form of an interrogation or a lecture.

Make sure all decision makers are present. Decision makers can be the users of a product or the budget holder, so make sure who they are before arranging to meet. Unless all decision makers are present your customer will not be able to reach a decision whether or not to buy. This would be a waste of everyone's time, and may be counterproductive in the long run if the information is conveyed second hand to the decision maker. You need to spend time beforehand checking these things out.

Aim not to sell the features of the product but to sell the benefits based on the customer's needs. The customer is probably not so interested in the mechanics of how the adjustable bed works: they want to know if it will help them get a good night's sleep or ease their back pain. By all means have all the relevant facts at your fingertips, but avoid getting caught up in the details of the product. Emphasise the benefits the customer will derive based on what they tell you about their needs, and encourage them to articulate these themselves.

If you listen and observe attentively people will often tell and show you how best to sell to them. At a conversational level, and if allowed and encouraged, people will express hopes, fears and frustrations. Allaying these by demonstration of good faith and descriptions of the product benefits can help to form a strong bond between the customer, you, and your product. Two areas into which many purchases fall are enhancing a situation or alleviating a problem. Buying a house or a car can be seen as enhancing and pleasurable. Buying a security system or insurance aim to avoid or alleviate a problem and may be seen as a necessary evil. Fear of loss seems to have a stronger motivational effect than hope of gain (Kahneman, Knatch and Thaler 1990), so allaying fear is often a strong motivator for positive prompt action. It is in any case a necessary prelude to building hope and optimism towards a mutually beneficial decision. Customers will often indicate areas of concern by their body language and gestures: for example, if they glance continually at a particular office door it may mean that they have tensions with a colleague, and this may be affecting their decision; or a fleeting frown when discussing a certain area indicates that you should persuade the customer to externalise any concerns.

Always be on the lookout for signs of irritation, impatience or boredom and take appropriate action, such as livening up your conversation or switching topics. Watch out also for your customer's choice of words; these will sometimes indicate their preferred learning style. Some people prefer to have information spoken to them; others prefer more visual presentations. To some customers the stylish appearance of your product will be more meaningful than your description of its efficiency. It is important to sell in the way your customers wish to buy.

Always do a full presentation. Even if your customer wants to take shortcuts, insist politely that they need to hear the full story, and explain that it really would be in their interests to do so.

Don't discuss money until you are ready. It is important to sell the product before attempting to negotiate a price. The price is irrelevant if the customer does not want the product: it is not a bargain even at half price. Salespeople themselves often make price an obstacle in their own minds, possibly because they may have over-reacted to some objections in the past and therefore anticipate that all customers are going to raise objections. This then becomes a self-fulfilling prophecy, which is why it is important for you to be confident in the quality of your product and the price it justifies (see the idea of appreciative inquiry on page 93). If a customer is focusing on price comparisons experienced salespeople will move the discussion to the area of benefits and the cost of buying an inferior product. This avoids getting into a ping-pong debate where each is trying to score points and no one wins.

The principles of price perception and price anchoring have been known and practised for centuries, because salespeople know that introducing a very high-priced version of the product will move customers' price acceptance upwards: the £10,000 version makes the £3,000 model more reasonable and probably a better choice than the 'cheap' £800 model. Much recent research has been carried out on price perception, drawing on work from other disciplines: for example, Kahneman and Tversky (2000) show the effectiveness of the principle with random numbers. They asked a group of participants to write down the last two digits of their social security number, and then guess the price of an item. Those with the higher number (say 65) were prepared to pay up to a third more for the item than those with the lower number (say 10). These numbers were entirely random and had no connection to the value of the object. This indicates that price is in many ways an arbitrary figure but that the way it is presented is hugely important. In another experiment, this time working with judges (for whom justice and wisdom are bywords), they slipped higher figures randomly into a conversation. They then asked the judges to consider which sentence they would pass on a convicted criminal for a particular scenario. The random numbers were shown to have effect of up to 30 per cent on the sentences the judges decided on. The lessons for you are that, by continually building value through the discussion and forming links and references to higher-priced objects, you can create a situation where the actual price comes as a pleasant surprise. Doing this skilfully without manipulation helps to balance the fact that the customer may be comparing your product to similar though cheaper products.

IN THE GRAND BAZAAR

In the Grand Bazaar of Istanbul a tourist approaches Samit and asks, 'How much is that bag?' 'Ten thousand lira,' Samit replies seriously. The tourist looks astonished. Samit bursts out laughing and explains kindly that he was only joking and that the bag is only 400 lira. The tourist looks relieved and smiles at Samit as she holds the bag. With one fell swoop and a fair degree of manipulation, Samit has anchored the price at a high level and made the tourist feel relieved and well-disposed towards him. Samit comes from generations of traders and has a store of innate and explicit understanding about human behaviour, none of which has ever made it into a book.

At some point your customer may raise objections and argue for a lower price (this is dealt with below). However, any negotiated reduction in price should involve a trade-off, such as the customer agreeing to purchase a larger quantity, or accept earlier delivery. They need to decide which beneficial feature to remove in return for a lower price. Doing this means you promote the strength and credibility of your product to show its inherent value.

Finally – always get a decision. Each presentation should have a specifically agreed purpose, whether it aims for the customer to make a decision to buy the product or acts as a fact-finding meeting where actions are agreed and allocated, and the date of the next meeting set. Do not leave the premises without a decision.

RELATING TO YOUR CUSTOMER

The presenting stage is where you form a relationship with your customer that you hope is going to result in a purchase. Do not take anything for granted or simply assume that your prospective customer is going to buy. They may already have checked out your product online or seen their friends using one similar to yours. Remember that your customers are experienced, knowledgeable persons. Also remember that they may genuinely wish to buy the product – yours or someone else's – but need you to talk them through it so they can make up their minds whether or not to buy from you.

A core principle of presenting is to develop a respectful relationship with your prospective customer, so they will come to have confidence that you are a trustworthy person who is not going to try to fool them with false information. You therefore need to focus on creating a context where you will conduct a respectful conversation that will be beneficial to both. Customers are likely to be irritated by manipulative attempts at over-friendliness. The presentation should be regarded as a professional, mutually beneficial collaboration with respect for personal boundaries. Most people will feel more comfortable and secure with this kind of relationship.

Never prejudge your customer. We often make judgements about their purchasing power depending on how they look or speak. Beware of sexist assumptions: for example, that women are not clever around cars, and that men do not do the washing. It can be tempting to think that someone in an old-fashioned jacket is not up-to-date with product information, or that a more mature person does not know the ins and outs of a computer. Looks can be deceptive. This is where you need to be self-critical and ask yourself, 'Why do I think this way? What has happened in my own life that leads me to think that this person may or may not be a potential customer?'

Even when the sale is a one-off, the relationship does not need to be. Selling has in fact become a form of relationship management where you aim for sustainable, pleasant and long-term collegiality.

THE METHODOLOGY OF PRESENTING

Presenting is best done by regarding it as a research process that involves a specific methodology with identifiable steps, as follows:

- establishing credibility and rapport;

- identifying your customer's needs;

- finding and presenting a solution (your product);

- taking action (the customer agrees to purchase).

Try to stick to the sequence even if your client wishes to jump ahead. Polite acknowledgement of questions with an assurance that you will soon be covering the issue usually demonstrates your professionalism and your confidence in the product. It is important not to seem to be controlling or disregarding of the client's concerns.

Establishing credibility

Establishing credibility involves the following:

- **Creating a context of trust:** This is your responsibility, not your customer's. Never be manipulative or try to persuade your customer to trust you so you can trick them, but make a genuine effort to establish dialogue. Above all, listen (see below). If you do not establish personal trust, the product benefits become irrelevant, because your customer may not believe they actually exist. You can also cite examples of other customers who have benefited from the product, which may help to allay anxieties about their making a poor purchasing decision.

FOCUSING ON SALIENT POINTS

I am Reggie and I sell paint to industrial customers. Sales books had told me that people buy from people they like and from people who are similar to themselves. In presentations I spent time recounting what I thought were interesting stories about myself and identifying common ground with my customer in hobbies and sports. This had negative effects in many cases. Some prospects would become irritated and cold. On reflection, I felt they needed to do this to keep our relationship at a sensible business-like distance. Other prospects would get into long story-telling sessions with me, until we realised we had burnt up the time available and came to an awkward finish with no result for either of us. Reflection-in-action led me to realise that I had misunderstood 'relationship building' and had moved away from a professional stance. Armed with this insight I worked hard to re-design my presentation around the customer's needs, our product and service support. I tried to let my personality manifest itself through a professional exploration of the customer and their needs, with me in a supporting, rather than starring role. As a result, and as a side benefit, I developed warm, respectful relationships with a number of customers.

- **Listening:** Listening involves several aspects. You need to be genuinely interested in other people. Many so-called dialogical encounters are in fact monological, where each person tries to grab as much airtime as possible to speak about themselves. Many conversations become two monologues speaking in turn (and sometimes not in turn as each interrupts the other). Some people seem to be naturals at listening: they are genuinely interested and curious about others' experiences and lives, while others need to learn how to listen. If this applies to you, try out some simple strategies: focus on making sense of what the person is saying, paraphrase it mentally and store it for future reference, or link what they say to a mnemonic system – for example, make up a story in your mind where you see them with the product you hope they are going to buy.

- **Demonstrating product knowledge:** There is a difference between 'just enough' forms of knowledge and expert knowledge. An expert demonstrates that they have in-depth knowledge of their subject; this is the kind you need. However, developing expert knowledge requires patience and application, in all walks of life (Sennett 2008).

- **Providing a track record:** Aim to demonstrate your own and your company's credibility with a brief history of both and the reason for selling this product. This is also an opportunity to show an understanding of the general situation pertaining to the client's industry or life situation. All this allows you to be taken seriously by the client.

- **Your manner and appearance**: Take care about how you look, speak and present yourself. Dress appropriately for the occasion. Go with what you feel is best for the context, and make sure that you feel comfortable yourself. Make sure you are nice to be with.

Present yourself as someone who enjoys their job and is enthusiastic for their product, knows what they are talking about, and has solutions and good ideas for your customer's needs. Enjoy yourself and share a joke, but never at the customer's or other people's expense.

Avoid the image of the brash, cocky salesperson that many customers would run a mile to avoid. Communicate what you have to say clearly and in a pleasant manner. This is not a competition; it is a dialogue where you explore your customer's needs and present them with a possible solution (your product) and other ideas. The process should be viewed as a shared, dialogical endeavour, and not as a contest where either you or the client wins. Rather than telling the client why they should buy your product, ask progressive questions that allow them to develop their answers more fully. Respect the fact that the client knows their own situation or business better than you do.

Identifying the customer's needs

Here are some tried and trusted dos and don'ts.

It may be necessary to investigate an area that is problematic for your customer in order to let them see the advantages that your product will bring or the problems it will help to avoid. While this might show the importance of the product and demonstrate the need for quick action it should not be done in a threatening way. If you are selling life insurance, emphasise the benefits to their family, not the tragedy of loss. It is however important to show the dangers of inaction.

Don't assume that you know what your customer needs or that your product is the one and only answer for their needs. They know what their needs are; it is your job to find this out. You can do this by asking them and creating a context where they feel comfortable speaking for and about themselves. Demonstrate respect at all times and ask questions without expecting concrete answers. Collingwood (1939) says there are no 'correct' answers in a conversation, only the 'right' ones that will keep the conversation open. Doing this, however, requires a specific attitude by you towards your customer. You need to see them as the person who knows their own business best, within their own contexts and circumstances. Your job is to find these things out by asking them, gently and professionally.

Don't talk at your customer, or talk for long periods of time, or harangue them about your product. Don't spend ages telling them all the features and benefits of your product. Steer the conversation so they feel encouraged to ask questions. A conversation is no fun if you are not taking part in it. It is crucial to confirm agreement at regular points. Objections should be exposed and settled. By removing objections and clarifying areas of doubt throughout the presentation you are helping to create a more positive view of your product. Ownership of it moves from the realms of possibility to reality. This helps to ensure that your customer is not accumulating doubts which they suddenly voice at the end of the conversation. Each element of the conversation can be a sub-conversation where you identify a need, meet the need, show a benefit and move on.

Do encourage your customer to talk about themselves and articulate what they hope to get out of the conversation with you. Listen carefully to what they have to say. As impediments are removed the language of the salesperson and customer should become more positive and action-oriented. The question moves gently from 'if' to 'when'. Ask permission to make notes, and do so to act as an aide-memoire (these notes can act as data when you come to writing up your project). Remember that you are not just looking to close the sale here and now, but are hoping to build a longer-term relationship. Reaching agreement to purchase may take several visits, though the first one may be enough. This can also vary according to the industry in which you are selling.

Do take your customer's identified needs seriously. Show respect and understanding at all times. They know what they want: what they don't know is whether you can give it to them.

So how you can demonstrate that you can meet your customer's needs?

Finding and presenting a solution to needs

This area itself includes key principles, including matching products to needs and dealing with objections.

Sometimes a product can meet all the identified needs of a customer, but more often not. You need to point out the benefits of your product to your customer and address their perpetual unvoiced question – 'What's in it for me?' Articulating the benefits enables your customer to develop an intellectual appreciation of the need for the product, and acts as the springboard to the more emotionally charged impetus to act, that is, agreement to purchase.

You are not serving your customer's needs merely by meeting their known requirements. You can introduce new features which can mean a great leap forward for your customer's business or life; for example, purchasing a home security system gives your customer a sense of safety, but adding the ability to check on their house remotely by a telephone application may be something they had not even considered but will greatly enhance their quality of life. This will be a convenient extra for your customer and enhance your company's income. You are now collaborating with your customer in developing both your businesses and contributing to your wellbeing.

Taking action

Taking action in this case refers to your customer making a decision to buy.

At this point some objections may remain. These often take the form, 'It's too expensive.' Sometimes customers will point out that they can get a similar product cheaper elsewhere. This often means, 'I would like it to be less expensive.' Acknowledge the importance of all objections, and point out the balance between problem and benefit. It is important now not to come over as glib or dismissive – take objections seriously and deal with them. Unless you do so your customer may maintain a mindset of a person who has already decided not to buy. Asking the right questions can help to keep the sale open. Listen carefully and show that you are reflecting seriously on the objection – and do so, don't only pretend to do so. Remember that during the presentation you are building the value of your product, and your customer should be seeing it deliver the value you are outlining at the designated price. Always focus on the central benefits of your product. People often make the decision to buy at an emotional and even tactile level. The appearance or feel of an object can be the deciding factor which is then justified post facto by a more cognitive analysis of benefits. It is important for the salesperson to appeal to both the emotional and intellectual processes of the decision maker. Remember that if there is dissonance between the customer's emotional desire for possessing the object and their inability to rationalise it intellectually they will experience a crisis. This often leads to their finding excuses not to close. The customer may not even recognise that they are doing it, and will often give a different reason for delaying their decision. You therefore need to investigate this further with your customer, because if it remains hidden and unchallenged it is not likely to be resolved. This is where skilful questioning and polite perseverance can bear fruit.

The point of taking action to purchase should be a smooth and natural part of the sales discussion. If the presentation has been inclusive and cooperative then the decision to act becomes a natural part of an ongoing shared endeavour. Your customer is less likely to put off a decision to buy if you have addressed all contentious issues earlier in the presentation. The decision should turn out to be the solution to a dilemma rather than lead to fear of creating a new one. It is reasonable to expect that details of purchasing can be completed at this point.

If your relationship has been mutually supportive your customer will feel a responsibility to you as much as you do to them. Their desire to own the product will be supported by their having confidence that they can explain their decision to buy to other possibly sceptical people (possibly co-workers, relatives or neighbours). A useful strategy is to find an opportunity for them to re-articulate to you, and themselves, what the benefits of the product are and how they picture themselves using it so they feel entirely satisfied with the outcome.

So, how do you test the validity of all these suggestions in your sales practices and possibly implement them?

How Do I Research Presenting in Action?

Here are some ideas about how you can research your practices of presenting. Remember, from a research perspective you need to show that you understand the principles of doing research, and, from a sales perspective, that you understand and can practise the principles of presenting. You also need to show that you can reflect critically on whether these approaches are right for you or whether to develop new ones.

A practical way of doing this is to regard your presentation as a genuinely collaborative exploration – that is, you and your customer are doing research together. This in itself enables you to evaluate whether you are building trust, listening properly and showing appreciation that your customer knows what they want but needs you to help them find the right product or service. You can do this by inviting your customer to join you in an action enquiry: you probably would not use this language but you would adopt the principles of doing research. You could ask your customer questions like these:

'What is your concern?' or 'What have you identified as an issue?' or 'What do you think you need?'

This helps you to understand your customer's needs.

By asking this kind of question you immediately put your customer in control of their situation, so they feel you are taking their matter seriously. They see that their concern or desire to find a solution is legitimate and not trivial. You show that you are not trying to control them, but are genuinely there to serve their needs. You and they explore the field together.

'Why is this an issue (or problem) for you?'

You explore the basics together.

Asking this helps you learn about your customer's context and concerns, which helps you to focus on their needs. If you are selling cosmetics, invite them to explain how they think using cosmetics would improve the quality of their life. If you are selling computer solutions, invite them to explain how a reliable backup technology service could help them save time and energy. Doing this helps you to imagine strategies to adapt your product to their needs. Encouraging another person to speak about their needs can be powerful and liberating: Freud found that encouraging clients to articulate what was going on for them helped them bring worries and anxieties to the surface. Look at the work of Polanyi (1958), who spoke about 'making the implicit explicit', and Freire (1995, 1993), who spoke about the importance of 'naming our world', putting language to experiences. The process would also help you and your customer to articulate your values to each other. Customers need to know that you share their values base, and are taking their concerns seriously.

'Can you explain to me/show me what is happening at the moment?'

This helps you to establish a baseline from which you can both proceed.

You ask your customer to show you their concern in action (in research language, you are inviting them to produce data). Possibly they will show you how difficult it is to climb the stairs in their home. You in turn suggest that your stair lift will be the ideal solution. They show you the peeling paint on their house. You encourage them to talk about their vision for their house and you explain how your exterior paint can help them realise their vision. Inviting your customer to identify and articulate their needs is a powerful strategy that also encourages them to regard the solution to their problem as their own: they have come up with their own answers. This is also a powerful pedagogical strategy used by teachers, nurses and all other professionals everywhere to encourage effective learning: they see the learner/customer in charge of their own learning. They emphasise that clients already have answers within themselves and can work them out if they have the confidence to do so (see also Brookfield 1987). It is your job to help them develop this confidence.

'What do you think you may be able to do about it?'

This involves their finding a solution (hopefully your product).

Work with your customer now to explore how your product can meet their needs. You must do this in a truly helpful way and never coercively or manipulatively, otherwise you could appear to be taking advantage of vulnerabilities. Encourage your customer to articulate for themselves what they see as the benefits to acquiring your product: the cosmetics will make them more attractive and desirable; the stair lift means they will no longer be barred from using the top floors of their homes. Encourage them to rationalise for themselves why they should acquire your product. This will enable them to justify purchasing it in the future and avoid potential buyer's remorse (regret at purchasing the product). You want to encourage buyer's delight.

As noted, the actual decision to purchase may involve some objections and reservations on the customer's part and negotiation for both parties. If customers say the price is too high explain that perceptions can be relative: yes, the product may not be the cheapest but delivers excellent benefits such as its dependability and low running costs. Many sales training schedules or books still teach that there are magic answers to objections. The best way to deal with objections is to anticipate them and build an answer to them into your presentation, and this means seeing the entire process as a form of research.

> 'What do you think buying this product will do for you?
> Can you imagine a world with it (or without it)?'

This involves your customer recording their reactions, which stand as quality data for your joint project.

The reasons for buying a product tend to fall under the heading of benefits obtained or problems avoided. Encourage your customer to think and talk about the benefits the product is going to contribute to their life and wellbeing. Don't try to tell them; just get them to talk about themselves. This is the basis of counselling practices, where we encourage people to articulate their dreams and imagine ways in which they can make the dreams come true. Many self-help texts work from this principle (for example, Cranfield 2007) as well as business texts (for example, Cockerell 2008).

> 'How will you check that it is working for you?
> How do you think it will change your life?'

This helps your customer, and you, to evaluate their decision to purchase and to objectify and rationalise it.

Most purchasing agreements state that customers have a cooling-off period before the purchase becomes final. This is probably the case with your sale too. Use this as an opportunity to encourage your customer to keep a record of their use of the product, perhaps in a daily or weekly diary or email record, where they record their experiences of using the product. In this way they will be able to see for themselves what their life was like before and after, and read the record for themselves. By doing this you help them firm up the intellectualisation of their purchase. They are able to see that, although the product was purchased partly from an emotional desire, they can actually see, at an intellectual level, the benefits it has brought them and the differences it has made to their lives. The records they keep could also act as data for their project, if they decide to do one, or yours (with their permission).

> 'What will you tell your friends and colleagues about your purchase?'

This helps your customer to disseminate their experiences of their purchase and get positive feedback from others, which enables them to feel fully confident and may lead to referrals.

Encourage your customer to say how they are going to share their pleasure in their purchase with friends and colleagues. Ask them to include you on their emails and social media messages so you both have a record of the purchase and subsequent use of the product. This can also act as a valuable resource that will help you follow up new leads for new sales.

If appropriate, you could invite your customer to write up your joint project for publication. Now, this would be a first in the scholarly literatures!

CASE STUDY

My name is Tracy and I work in the City of London finance district. My company supplies financial analytic systems to investment banks. I attempt to be approachable and collaborative in dealing with clients. However, on later analysing my presentations, I found that some clients would see my less aggressive approach as an opportunity to take control of the meeting. I found that I was attempting to field a barrage of fast questions with no opportunity to develop my answers. One downside of this was that I was forced only to offer solutions to immediate problems as they were presented and not move on to show greater potential and added value with extra products.

After reflecting on this I decided to try different strategies which would allow shared leadership during presentations. At the beginning of presentations I would set out a suggested agenda, which included updates on the latest technology that would enhance my client's competitiveness. When I felt that the client was trying to become controlling and dominant I would disengage by making my body language less amenable by leaning back and reducing eye contact. I would pause before answering questions that were being fired too quickly and speak more slowly and quietly so the client would need to pay close attention. This balanced out the power relationship more effectively and I would ask a question at the end of my replies to build up a more egalitarian and collaborative relationship.

Although some of this felt a bit competitive I considered it was sometimes necessary in an aggressive and demanding environment. My notes showed that presentations had become more interactive with a better balance of questions and answers, and my figures showed that my sales of added value products rose.

Summary

Chapter 6 is about taking action in the research process. This is when practitioners decide to do something about a social situation with a view to improving it. Doing so involves reflection in action and a critical awareness of change processes. Action research requires practitioners to exercise their agency in order to influence processes of change, emphasising the importance of dialogue. Taking action in research is linked with presenting, where we look at the characteristics of the sales process and the importance of understanding relationships as a core methodological feature.

Chapter 7 now focuses on evaluating your research and assessing whether it has helped you improve your understanding and practice of selling.

Chapter 7

Evaluating Your Research: Consolidating and Developing

This chapter is about evaluating your action research, that is, checking whether you have improved your sales practice through researching it in action; and whether you are providing a high-quality product or service and a consistently high-quality customer experience.

Evaluation is also an intrinsic part of the consolidating and developing phase of the sales process, where you build on the mutually beneficial and trusting relationship you have already developed with your customer. You check that all orders are correct and delivery is arranged, and provide after-care support. All promises are kept and exceeded where possible. These are essential elements for ensuring customer satisfaction, which contributes to building customer loyalty, securing repeat business and attracting a wider clientele through the customer's own referrals and recommendations. Evaluation is essential to your work because it contributes to building sustainable relationships and the development of customer-oriented professional learning. Your evaluation can also help you see the potential implications of your learning for developing new practices in sales. It strengthens the idea of evaluation as a collaborative endeavour by people who are involved in shared practices.

The chapter covers these sections.

- What does evaluating involve?

- What are the principles of consolidating and developing?

- How do I research consolidating and developing in action?

What Does Evaluating Involve?

Action research in itself is a form of evaluation. You identify something that needs attention, do an initial stocktake of what the situation is now, imagine ways of improving it, implement the imagined solutions, keep records of what happens and come to some provisional conclusions about whether it has improved. You are evaluating your work as you do it.

Evaluation is essential in practices because it means showing that you have done what you say you have done. In professional practices you can show that you are demonstrating accountability, to yourself, your customers and your company. You also evaluate what you are doing in order to learn from experience, and you use the learning to improve your performance and practice as and when necessary.

Evaluation is a core methodological aspect of doing research, because, as noted in Chapter 1, research is about making knowledge claims. Your knowledge claims could be that you have improved your sales practice, raised your professionalism and brought added value to your company. However, as soon as you say you have done something, someone somewhere is bound to say, 'Show me'. This is a fair request because you cannot say you have done something without producing evidence to show that they can believe you. You also need to know what counts as evidence (see below). By producing evidence you can demonstrate and strengthen the validity of your knowledge claims, which can also greatly strengthen the legitimacy of your work, and enable you to use your knowledge for the wider good.

Here we consider two points:

1.   some general issues about evaluation;

2.   some practicalities of generating evidence.

SOME GENERAL ISSUES ABOUT EVALUATION

Here are some general points to think about when discussing evaluation.

The purposes of evaluation

Evaluation is about establishing the value of something: it is based on the idea of 'value', that is, what is of value. There are different forms of evaluation, which involve different processes. All are equally useful in their place, and you need to decide which is right for you. The form of evaluation you choose depends on your values, how you position yourself in your research and how you choose to tell your story. Kushner (2000) makes the point that 'the values of the evaluator are written directly into the methodology and in which, above all, the evaluator is expected to discover a personal voice' (p. 108).

Evaluation is linked with aims and processes: You ask, 'What was the overall aim of the project? Was it achieved, and how was this done?' Evaluation is therefore linked with the idea of 'the good': you aim to achieve something you believe is desirable and what you consider is 'good'. The idea of 'the good' is linked with quality: you consider your work to be of good quality. This area can be tricky, because different people have different ideas of what counts as good (that is, they have different values). Al Capone's ideas of what counted as good may have been different from those of Gandhi – but both shared the same values about good social order although they used different means to achieve it. Evaluation is full of banana skins because it involves making judgements about personal commitments and finding ways of testing the validity of both the commitments and the judgements. This can be difficult because we need to remain critical and remember that whatever we say is said from within our own situatedness and experience. It involves asking ourselves, 'Is this what I think, or what my culture/partner/boss has told me to think?' or even, 'Is this what they want me to say?'

Positionalities in evaluation: external and internal evaluation

Broadly speaking, there are two positionalities in evaluation – external and internal (though you can have a mix-and-match situation too). External evaluation is where an external evaluator considers what other people are doing and makes judgements about it. They ask, 'What were the aims of the project? Were they achieved?' Internal evaluation is where the insider practitioner(s) themselves considers what they are doing and makes judgements about it. They ask, 'What were my/our aims for the project? Did I/we achieve them?'

Formative and summative evaluation

There are also two forms of evaluation – formative and summative (you can mix these forms too). Formative evaluation is evaluation on the go. You stop periodically and check whether you are achieving your aims. If not, you move in a different direction. Also, the aims themselves may change as a result of the evaluation process: they emerge as participants' understandings develop: 'the notion that an evaluation can be designed at the outset and then pursued relentlessly to its conclusions is to misunderstand the emergent nature of theory' (Kushner 2000: 87). Summative evaluation is where you evaluate at the end of a project. You look back on the entire experience and ask questions about what has happened and whether it has been successful.

Criteria

Making judgements about something means identifying criteria to guide your thinking (see Chapter 5).

There are different kinds of criteria too. There are objective, product-oriented criteria, often phrased in the form of objectives, outcomes and competencies: this links strongly with the idea of technical rationality. For example, the Green IT Awards (2013) propose the following criteria for products in different categories:

Commercial relevance and impact

Commercial viability of product or solution:

- *potential for financial success;*
- *overall practicality and usefulness;*
- *adaptability to market.*

Customer care, judged on:

- *evidence of an embedded progressive strategy to improve the customer's experience;*
- *customer satisfaction levels;*
- *value for money;*
- *quantified research on brand perception.*

Decisiveness, characterised by and judged on:

- *making decisions faster than competitors;*
- *committing resources and manpower to a Green product, solution or practice.*[1]

---

1   See http://www.caddealer.com/greenitawards/index.php?page=judging.

However, Kushner (2000) makes the point that these kinds of objectified, externally created criteria are not always relevant to the personalised, context-specific forms of evaluation that are conducted by practitioners in workplaces. Schön and Rein (1994) agree: in offering a critique of traditional forms of establishing criteria in policy analysis they say:

> ... the evaluation movement has never succeeded in resolving several of its central problems. The first of them is the problem of defining criteria for evaluation. By what standards should a program be evaluated? The conventional answer is that a program should be evaluated by its purposes. But most programs have multiple, conflicting, and evolving purposes that are discovered only in the context of carrying out the evaluation (p. 12).

This idea of recognising the complexities of different interactions gave rise to the idea of process criteria, which refer to descriptions of the progress people are making in a particular situation. An example can be found in Stenhouse (1975): he originated the idea of a process curriculum, which emphasises the importance of interactions among people. So instead of identifying specific outcomes and performance indicators of good practice, process evaluation examines and makes judgements about the quality of those interactions. Elliott (1991) sees this view as core to action research. He emphasises that practitioners need to be involved in evaluation processes, as do Schön and Rein (1994), who say that criteria should be related to living practices:

> If policy academics want to build a better understanding of policy practice in a way useful to practitioners, as well as appropriately rigorous, then they must not bypass the research in which practitioners are already engaged. If they disregard what practitioners already know or are trying to discover, they are unlikely either to grasp what is really going on or to succeed in getting practitioners to listen to them (p. 193).

The idea of process evaluation is core to action research. As noted, the entire process of action research may be seen as a form of evaluation. You ask, individually or collectively, how you can improve a particular situation, gather data and generate evidence to show the processes involved. You make judgements about whether or not you have improved it, as part of the process of testing the validity of your emerging knowledge claims prior to disseminating your findings to other people.

CHANGING CRITERIA

My name is Omar and I work in sales of kitchen refurbishments direct into the home. When I first entered sales I realised I had to set my own targets, write them down and compare them to actual outcomes. I first set the criteria of making enough contacts. This is because I was told repeatedly that 'sales is a numbers game'. I usually achieved my targets in terms of contacts, but my conversion rate to appointments was not high, so I moved my criteria to achieving more appointments. My next criterion was to turn a greater ratio into sales. This reflected my growth and development as a salesperson. If I had tried to bypass any of these criteria, I do not think I would have succeeded at any particular stage and moved on to the next. By the time I identified consolidating and developing as an area in which to improve I felt quite confident in my sales role.

Different questions at different times

When you decide to do a formal evaluation of your research, you ask different questions at different times. At the beginning of your evaluation you ask questions like these:

- What do we want to evaluate?

- Why do we want to evaluate it?

- Who are we evaluating for?

- How will we evaluate?

- Who will do the evaluation and do we have the right skills and knowledge?

- When will we do it?

- What resources will we need, including outside support?

- What will we do with the information we get?[2]

---

2   Adapted from the Charities Evaluation Services, available at http://www.ces-vol.org.uk.

As you move through the evaluation you ask questions about what you are looking for. For example, you may be looking for quantitative information, in which case you ask questions of the kind:

- How many people were involved in delivering this product?

- How many sales were made?

- How often are inventories taken?

If you are looking for qualitative information you ask, for example:

- What did the customer say about the purchasing experience?

- What does the feedback show about the efficiency of the finance department?

- How can we use the feedback from online customers when designing a new website?

When you get to the end of your evaluation you ask questions about what you are evaluating, such as:

- Was the practice being evaluated successful? If so, how?

- Did our evidence show that we had improved our practices?

- Did we as practitioners demonstrate respect for other people's opinions?

You also ask questions about the evaluation process itself. You ask:

- Did we do the job properly? Could we have done it differently?

- Can we explain why we asked particular kinds of questions rather than others?

- Do we demonstrate methodological rigour?

Doing evaluation involves a good deal more than what is outlined here, and many books are available on the topic. However, the advice so far should help to get you started.

SOME PRACTICALITIES OF GENERATING EVIDENCE

We now move to the practicalities of generating robust evidence. It is not enough simply to produce data to show that you have improved your work or managed your project effectively; you also have to turn the data into evidence. This practice of demonstrating methodological rigour is central to achieving academic recognition.

It involves knowing:

- the difference between data and evidence;

- how to generate evidence from the data and use it to ground knowledge claims;

- how to test the validity of your knowledge claims;

- different forms of validity;

- the difference between validity and legitimacy.

The difference between data and evidence

In Chapter 5 we said that data are those pieces of information you gather using different methods. We suggested that you could look for different types of data using a range of methods. You would keep your data in a data archive and sort and re-sort it into categories as preparation for analysing and interpreting it, as we discuss now.

Analysing and interpreting data
As part of the data gathering process, decide on and establish criteria. A useful strategy is to revisit your values: for example, the values of efficiency, punctuality, good conduct and professional behaviour become consistent points of reference. You could say that your values become the criteria by which you judge quality, as they emerge in practice (McNiff 1989, 2010, 2013a).

If you look through your data archive with your values-as-criteria in mind, you could identify those pieces of data that show the values/criteria in action. You can show, for example, an email from a customer thanking you for prompt delivery of the goods (prompt delivery is a value that acts as a criterion); or a videotape of you and a colleague practising interviewing techniques through role play (careful listening is a value that acts as a criterion); or a memo from your company manager congratulating you on the number of sales). These data will act potentially as evidence.

However, although this is a core methodological point, in practice it can be tricky (as noted earlier) because different people have different values, so you need to negotiate your own values with those of the other people in the encounter, including your customer and colleagues.

How to generate evidence from the data and use it to ground knowledge claims

Establishing criteria is essential for generating evidence. When you say, 'I have done something', and people say, 'Show me', you search your data archive for those pieces of data that show an identified value (for example, participation or customer care) in action. As noted, these data can take a range of forms: an email from a customer thanking you for a good meeting, accompanied by an order; a memo from your manager congratulating you on your high level of sales. You drag these pieces of data, in whole or part, out of your data archive and drop them into a new archive called 'evidence archive'. The pieces of data remain the same but their status changes: they become evidence.

Appreciating how this works at a procedural level is important when you are telling someone about your research or writing a report, and ensures that your ideas and writing are taken seriously. It is essential if you wish to demonstrate the validity (truthfulness) of what you are saying. When people say, 'Show me why I should believe you', you can produce the evidence they require. This helps you to ground your claims to knowledge and show that they are authentic.

In action research you can use quantitative and qualitative forms of data and evidence, for example:

- spreadsheets to show the rise in number of orders since you began using a more customer-centred approach;

- video clips of yourself in conversation with colleagues to show how you are practising your listening skills;

- emails and tweets to show how you are finding new customers and maintaining links with existing ones.

Over time you aim to build a strong and sustainable evidence base. Showing this to other people justifies your claim to be conducting evidence-based practice.

A further step in the validating process is to show that other people agree that your evidence is robust (that is, your evidence will withstand critique), that you have exercised methodological responsibility in showing the procedures for generating evidence, and that the work you refer to is ethically and practically sound. You do this as follows.

How to test the validity of your knowledge claims

You can get the agreement of other parties that your claims to knowledge are authentic and credible using several techniques. Some of the most important are:

- identifying critical friends and inviting their feedback;

- convening a validation group;

- negotiating what counts as quality in sales practice;

- negotiating what counts as quality in research practice.

Critical friends
Right from the beginning of your research you should invite two or more people to act as critical friends. Their job is to offer you feedback on what you are doing. They can be the same people for the duration of the research or different ones as the research proceeds. They should be supportive and critical, that is, point out where you may be in error or need to re-think something. They are your allies. You can draw your critical friends from your work colleagues, customers, friends and family, or other course members if you are on a formal course of studies.

Validation group
A validation group consists of four to ten people (or more – this number varies with your context) who can give you balanced and critical advice on how you

are getting on. Their job is to give you advice about the quality of your research and the validity of your provisional knowledge claims. You should convene a validation group at significant points in your research; for example, when you are preparing to submit a progress report or your final report or dissertation. Your critical friends may or may not be part of this group – whatever is right for you and your circumstances. Everyone should be supportive, but also give you honest feedback that will help you improve the quality of your work and engage with the following issues.

- *What counts as quality in sales practice?* You can show people how you judge quality in your sales practice. This involves negotiating what counts as evidence, which in turn includes identifying the most appropriate criteria for the job. For example, you can produce evidence to show that you have facilitated a good customer experience. The evidence takes the form of you and your customer negotiating and living your values in your practice.

- *What counts as quality in research practices?* You can also explain, at a methodological level, how you have taken those same values as criteria and standards of judgement: for example, you explain how you identified the values of honouring your customer and their involvement in the sales process as the criteria and standards that you and they consider contribute to a quality experience. This means that, when you analyse what you are doing at a methodological level, you can produce evidence of the epistemological, methodological and ethical robustness of your research design and implementation.

Different forms of validity

You should be aware that different researchers speak about different forms of validity. Here are some of the most common forms.

- Catalytic validity: this communicates the idea that the experience of a study can help people move to new, more productive forms of thinking.

- Construct validity: this refers to the idea that a researcher already had established models and constructs about the topic they are researching. They therefore need to check whether there are better ways of understanding a situation than imposing their existing constructs on it.

- Face validity: the situation appears a matter of commonsense: you can take it at face value.

- Ironic validity: you do not take things at face value but interrogate underlying assumptions.

- Rhizomatic validity: this refers to the interconnectedness of people and the power of a study for influencing new directions.

However, we authors believe (as outlined above) that establishing quality and demonstrating validity are grounded in a researcher's ontological values (McNiff 2013a). Similarly, Feldman (2003) argues that validity has to be linked with one's moral purposes in the world. We argue that personal validity may be demonstrated through showing that one has realised one's values in practice; and social validity may be demonstrated through appreciating that other people may not share our values, so values need to be negotiated, especially if they are to be seen as criteria in methodological matters.

Therefore, evaluation processes really do need to be collaborative. When we evaluate practices we need to bear in mind that practices are seldom conducted in solitary confinement: they are usually social. Evaluation of practices needs to be social too. Cockerell (2008), who worked at Disney World, points out the value of this kind of collaborative mindset. He tells the story of how, during the 'difficult days following 9/11' when numbers of visitors diminished and 'executives and managers were desperately looking for ways to cut costs', he involved all members of staff in coming up with good ideas. He writes:

> Their response was extraordinary. Some of them came up with a process to make the bus routes more efficient, thereby saving on gas and cutting down on labour costs. Others suggested landscaping changes: mowing the grass less often or planting flowers only in the visible places where Guests could enjoy them. ... The ideas saved a few hundred dollars here and a few thousand there, adding up to enough reductions to keep us going at full speed without laying off one person (p. 184).

It is not a question of 'I' so much as 'we', that is, how do we evaluate our practices together? How do we improve them for mutual benefit? If you can show how you have conducted a collaborative evaluation as a natural part of your sales practice, you will again have scored a first in the scholarly field.

A new question now arises: How will conducting my evaluation convince my management team to take me more seriously as a practitioner researcher? This involves issues of power, and foregrounds the differences between validity and legitimacy.

The difference between validity and legitimacy

There is a difference between validity and legitimacy. Validity is to do with matters of truthfulness, and legitimacy is to do with matters of power. When you say, 'My claim is valid' you are saying, 'You can believe what I am saying.' It is something else when you say, 'You should accept what I am saying.'

Matters of legitimacy

Establishing the legitimacy of knowledge claims moves the discussion into whether or not your claims should be accepted by others. This can be tricky because some people may not agree to your claims being accepted, in spite of the most rigorous evidence base, or for you to be seen as a knowledge producer.

For example, say you are a member of a company that has used tried and trusted methods for prospecting. You start to use social media in imaginative ways, learning from other industries. However, your sales manager does not see this as a legitimate exercise, as you are breaking with the way things have been done previously. It takes some time for the validity of the exercise in terms of its success rate to let it become an accepted and legitimate form of activity for the company. This is often the experience of practitioner–researchers across the professions (and throughout history): they show the validity of what they are doing yet it takes time for their ideas to become accepted and granted legitimacy. The experience is often related to power, since the old guard in an organisation or institution may often resist innovation, and it takes time to change habits of mind. On the bright side, it can be a great opportunity for you to show the potentials of your research for improving institutional and organisational practices and contribute to the development of your company as a learning organisation.

The issues outlined so far in this chapter are part of the vigorous debates that take place in academic studies, especially in terms of the democratisation of knowledge and theory. We said in Chapter 1 that many academics do not want to let go of their established power. They still maintain the idea that research should be judged in relation to the criteria of social science research, usually those of generalisibility, replicability and objectivity (see page 40). More forward-thinking academics tend to embrace newer forms of enquiry and scholarship, where practice is seen as both the site of research and the focus of the research (that is, you research your practice in action). In this kind of research the criteria for judging validity change. A practitioner can show, for example, that they are living their values in practice, and produce evidence to show this in action. It has taken time for such new forms to be accepted in the academic world, but they are now firmly established. The implications for you as a salesperson are that you would claim legitimacy for your research that shows how you are developing collaborative practices with your customers and colleagues, or how you are developing a view of sales as dialogical relationship. By doing this you can have significant influence in relation to your organisation and actually contribute to changing the culture (see Chapter 8).

Now let's consider what is involved in consolidating and developing, and how this phase of the sales process constitutes a form of evaluation.

What Are the Principles of Consolidating and Developing?

Commonly agreed aims and anticipated outcomes are as follows.

AIMS OF CONSOLIDATION AND DEVELOPING

The aim of consolidation and developing is to develop your company's ongoing relationship with the customer, leading to further opportunities for both. It is essential to ensure that your customer's purchasing experience is not let down by quality of aftercare: failure to deliver or support could tarnish your own and the company's reputation, and possibly also lead to loss of future opportunities. The aim is also to encourage repeat business and referrals through ensuring a good customer experience and quality aftercare.

ANTICIPATED OUTCOMES

You anticipate that your customer will be delighted with their purchase so they will become repeat customers. They will also tell their friends and colleagues, so your client base will expand through their recommendations.

Here are the key principles of the consolidation process.

THE PRINCIPLES OF CONSOLIDATING

In Chapter 6 we noted that, during the presentation process, and having agreed prices, completed the order form and arranged delivery, it is now important in this consolidating phase to re-sell your product. You can do this through revisiting the benefits your customer will derive, and encouraging them to articulate these: you do this so that, having taken the final step to purchase at an emotional level, they now re-sell themselves on the benefits of the product at an intellectual level. This is important for several reasons:

- You avoid buyer's remorse: this is when your customer frets over the decision they have made, possibly under pressure from third parties. It may also help them when they have to justify their purchase to a friend or colleague. You can help them by encouraging them to repeat the benefits of the purchase for themselves. This consolidates the decision into a joint emotional and intellectual action; once a customer can rationalise their actions at an intellectual level, it makes it easier to commit emotionally and justify their purchase in their own terms. They can reassure themselves of the wonderful time they are going to have achieving market edge through using their new software system, driving their new car or wearing their new shoes.

- Articulating something consolidates it in the mind. Your customer needs to hear themselves saying that they are pleased with their purchase. They are confident in having made the right choice, of product and of salesperson.

- When you part company, they will continue to be excited about their purchase: no regrets or recriminations – just delight that they have got what they wanted, at a good price, and with a great experience to be remembered for the next time.

It is your responsibility to follow up on all organisational matters: submitting the order, confirming delivery dates, negotiating with colleagues in different organisational departments (orders, finance, delivery) and ensuring that everything will go as planned. Check that any promises you have made with your customer about delivery dates or special requests are achievable, and that the company will be able to meet them (do not make any promises without checking with the company first). All logistical matters must be in place to ensure timely delivery and correct ordering.

Aim to connect with your customer immediately after the purchase, whether by telephone, email or letter. Thank them for their business and assure them that everything is in hand. Remind them of the benefits of their purchase to consolidate the justification of their decision. Repeat that you have arranged delivery and that their goods will arrive on the agreed date.

BUILDING VALUE THROUGH TRUST

My name is Mikal. When I started to sell our ventilation system to businesses I took care to know every benefit and technical detail. As I spent more time with existing customers I came to realise that the product or artefact itself was only part of what the customer wanted to buy. The backup service, regular advice about how to conform to new regulations and passing on new development information formed a large part of the iceberg. My problem was that, although the customer wanted this, they often did not see it at the pre-sale point and would focus only on technical points and price. This meant I quickly had to reach a point where the prospective customer would trust me enough to allow me to bring the support aspect into the equation. I felt that every aspect of my behaviour contributed to this trust. From the moment I drove into their car park, walked into their reception and said hello, I was on show for my company. The learning from developing relationships with existing customers looped back to my very first contact with prospects.

Paying attention to customers' needs at this point is essential because you can build up a whole new client base from one person. You can ask them to post a comment online or send tweets to colleagues and friends: a good customer experience can lead to repeat business with the same customer, and potentially to a wider customer circle. A satisfied customer who is influential in their industry may extend your collaborative partnership by doing some of your prospecting for you. This is important whether you are contributing to a company's business, or building up your own. In some very competitive industries, customers may not want to share helpful information with rivals but may not object to your naming them as being among your satisfied customers. In consolidating you aim to add value to your product, because your customer speaks about your product not only as a product but also as offering a solution to their identified needs. If you work with a larger service company you can enhance this experience by involving customer relations staff, and this element of teamwork can greatly enhance your customer's experience.

Ensuring good follow-up avoids alienating your customer. A lost customer means ripples of discontent and negativity that can lose other customers and make recruiting new ones more difficult. Bad news travels faster than good news.

There is research evidence to show that customers feel less positively than salespeople about the potential ongoing nature of the relationship.[3] You can combat this and build up your customer's confidence by treating them, and encouraging them to treat you, as fellow human beings: they appreciate being able to discuss problems with knowledgeable salespeople and being reassured that they are making the right purchasing choices. Notwithstanding the traditional advice to 'always be closing', there may be times when the customer wants a person-to-person discussion about more general matters. Responding to this can move you out of the realms of the opportunistic seller to a broader and deeper mutually supportive relationship.

You can realise these principles effectively through researching your practice and considering some of the following ideas.

How Do I Research Consolidating and Developing in Action?

This section offers ideas about how you can research your practices of consolidating and developing in action, referring again to the critical questions on pages 42–3. From an action research perspective you are showing that you understand the principles of evaluating and from a sales perspective that you can effectively consolidate and develop the relationship with your customer. You appreciate what is involved in generating evidence from the data, and the need to identify criteria and standards of judgement; you use this understanding when you generate evidence from your data about your sales practices.

FORM OF QUESTIONS ASKED

At this point you ask evaluative questions. These kinds of questions enable you to take stock of practical and logistical aspects by ticking off 'to do' tasks, and checking whether, say, delivery schedules have been arranged and accounts organised and sent out. They also give you feedback about relational aspects and help you check whether you are achieving your aims and contributing to

---

3   See page 6 of the Forum Corporation Report online at http://www.forum.com/_assets/download/276d15f6-ff6f-42c1-9d09-eaab3db3cc4d.pdf.

a good customer experience. This kind of feedback is invaluable in the short term because it allows you and others to ensure that you and your company are operating at maximum performance level. In the longer term it can be used as strong evidence to show that you have achieved a high level of performance and are prepared to hold yourself accountable for what you are doing.

Here is a generic action plan that helps you evaluate your practice at a local level, such as during a sales encounter with a customer, at the consolidation and developing stage of the sales process; and also at an organisational level, where you show that you are achieving a high level of professionalism and are a valuable asset to your company.

HOW DO I EVALUATE MY PRACTICES IN CONSOLIDATING?

As noted, you can use the consolidating stage of the sales process as an opportunity to evaluate your performance during the business meeting. You could ask your customer for feedback about what you did that led them to agree to purchase, or, in cases where they did not agree to purchase, whether you did or said anything that influenced their decision negatively. You would seek feedback about the entire experience wherever possible: from your initial contact to the closing of the sale.

You can also check with other people in your company whether they have enjoyed the experience of working with you and whether you could do things differently or better in the future. Did you fill out the order forms correctly? Did you stick with the agreed schedule? If you are writing up your project report it is helpful to get this feedback in writing, by email or on tape, or in some durable form, so you can use it, with appropriate permissions, as valuable data.

WHY IS IT IMPORTANT TO EVALUATE?

Evaluation is central to establishing the quality of your service and your professionalism. You show that you are not simply doing the job, but reflecting and actively critiquing what you are doing, that is, you are turning yourself into an extended professional. You are demonstrating responsibility to yourself, your organisation and your profession by locating your capacity for critical reflection at the heart of your practice. You are showing how you are trying to live your values in practice and encouraging others, including colleagues and customers, to live theirs too. At a methodological level you would be able to analyse how you had transformed your values into dynamic criteria and standards by which you can judge the quality of your practice.

You could draw on many of the important conceptual frameworks mentioned in this book to show the importance of evaluation: for example, the ideas of Mezirow (2009) (see page 135) who emphasises the need for transformative thinking and of Schön (1983) who speaks of the need for reframing as the basis for critical thinking (Schön and Rein 1994) (see page 136). You can also make the point that doing action research is in itself an evaluation process, where you trace the steps that require you to show how you hold yourself accountable for what you are doing.

HOW DO I GATHER DATA?

Gathering data is an important part of an evaluation process, so you can show how the situation develops as you take action. During the consolidating and developing stage invite your customer to give you feedback about their experience: for example, you check continually whether you are being clear about any aspects of the product or service, and whether they wish to ask any further questions or need further information from you. This tells them they can rely on you to make sure they are fully informed at all times. Many people feel awkward about asking obvious or seemingly trivial questions. Anticipate this and reassure them that you are taking everything they say seriously. Make notes as you go on your notepad; people tend to feel more comfortable when they see you have written something down and are not relying on your memory. Reassure them also that they can contact you at any point after your meeting to check on any details you or they may have overlooked.

Aim also to get your customer's feedback after the sale. You can send them a questionnaire, or ask them to email you with a short comment on the meeting. Get their permission to use this in public (assure them that they can remain anonymous if they wish). Ask their permission to put their comments on your company's website and in your advertising literature. Recommendations from real-life customers can go a long way to attracting new customers and sustaining existing business relationships.

For your future reference, use your customer's perspective to view your own product and company through their critical eyes. Are they positive about what and how you have delivered the product? Would they recommend it, and you, to others? A common strategy these days is to invite online customer feedback using the words, 'I would recommend this product to a friend.' Are there any issues they would have liked handled differently? This kind of critique can help strengthen your service and image, as well as show that you are willing to hold yourself accountable for your work. This is a real marker of professionalism.

WHAT NEW ACTIONS CAN I TAKE?

Remind yourself of what you need to do during the consolidation and developing stage, and think of innovative practices that will make the experience more valuable for all. Key points to bear in mind are:

- Aim to turn the purchasing event into a dialogue where you and your customer discuss the benefits of purchasing your product, and steer the conversation so they can repeat the benefits for themselves.

- Always encourage your customer to link the cost–benefit analysis of the purchase to the benefits of using the product and the pleasure this brings. This helps them take ownership at different intellectual and emotional levels.

- Keep in mind the psychology underpinning these aspects, and how emotional elements underpin even the most hard-nosed businesses. Appadurai (1988), for example, speaks about people's close relationships with things, and Baudrillard (2005) explains how people's possessions give them symbolic power and value. Get your customer to talk about how good their ownership of the product will make them feel.

These are not manipulative techniques. They are everyday strategies used in many social encounters that help others feel good about themselves. When you buy something from Marks & Spencer, the counter staff always make a positive comment about your purchase, which makes you feel you have made a wise choice.

Reinforce the positive experience of the sale through a follow-up letter. Positive reinforcement is a key element of encouraging loyalty and repeat business, which is partly why supermarkets and other businesses create loyalty bonus schemes. Thank your customer for their business and for putting their trust in you and your company. Restate the benefits of your product for their wellbeing, and express hopes for a developing relationship. Offer yourself as point of contact at any time (make sure you have left a business card or two with your customer). You can also make a telephone call as a follow-up the day after the sales meeting, but keep everything light and avoid overkill.

Make contact with your own organisation to ensure all the things you have promised will happen. Remember not to make promises without checking that you can be certain of delivery dates, that support and advice will be available, and that your set-up and instructions are followed up effectively.

If your purchaser is not the user of your product and has purchased it on behalf of someone else, arrange for the user to have direct access to ongoing advice and support.

HOW DO I ENSURE I AM ON THE RIGHT TRACK AT ALL POINTS?

It is at this point that you need to evaluate your evaluation, with a view to ensuring that you have covered all angles and not left anything to chance. Check you have addressed the following issues:

- Have you interrogated everything you have done to make sure it is in the interests of your customer and of yourself?

- Have you done a full analysis of your customer's needs? Have you met them?

- Have you introduced new ideas about the benefits and features of the products or services?

- Have you agreed with your customer to take action?

- Have you consolidated the decisions made during the meeting?

- Have you achieved all the pre-agreed tasks for the meeting?

- Have you got the answers you were looking for? Have they given you insights about possible new directions?

You also need to ask yourself questions about the methodological rigour of your evaluation process. Have you done the following:

- Gathered appropriate data?

- Identified appropriate criteria and standards for judging which data may be transformed into evidence?

- Linked these criteria to the values and practices of selling – for example that you have demonstrated care for your customer, efficient delivery and support service, punctual return of telephone calls.

- Created a robust evidence base using the data you have selected? Can you show your values/criteria in action in all aspects of your evidence?

- Kept records of feedback from critical friends for the duration of your research?

- Produced reports and other feedback from your validation group to show that they are reasonably satisfied that your claims are believable and trustworthy?

TRIANGULATION

The concept of triangulation is important. Its history goes back to early mathematics, but it is used today in a range of areas, including research. In basic terms it refers to the experience of thinking about or looking at something from at least three different perspectives, for example, when different persons offer feedback on the quality of data and evidence from different perspectives. It is important to get multiple perspectives on events to avoid unwarranted bias.

By undertaking these kinds of practices and writing them into your reports, you can show how you have taken stock of what you are doing on a systematic basis, and can be reasonably confident that others can take you seriously.

HOW WILL I DEVELOP NEW PRACTICES IN LIGHT OF MY EVALUATION?

Your evaluation can help you develop new practices in a range of ways. For example:

- You can strengthen areas in which you feel you are already competent, and focus more attention on weaker areas.

- You can develop greater collaborative practices in your organisation by asking colleagues for feedback about your practice. Do not be disappointed if some of the features appear to be negative. It is important to face up to the truth whatever it may look like. By developing such practices you can establish and strengthen the idea of sales as a learning practice, and your organisation as a learning organisation.

- You can, if appropriate, contribute to transforming a competitive culture into a more collegial and supportive one. While each person in the organisation needs to show that they are pulling their weight, they can do so without negative behaviours or harsh words.

CASE STUDY

My name is Henry. I sell tractors and farm machinery and have a good success rate in getting appointments. A healthy percentage of my presentations result in sales. On studying my sales figures I was concerned to see that the percentage of cancellations I get are higher than others in my company. I decided to investigate this by evaluating different stages of my sales process. I identified the consolidation and development stage of the sales process because this appeared to be the weak link in an otherwise strong chain. I first needed to decide on an approach to evaluating my consolidation practices.

My first action was to telephone each customer who cancelled to tell them how sorry I was that they had done so and ask for their help by feeding back to me the reasons why they cancelled. A reason that arose more than others was of delays in delivery times. When I queried this with the customer it became apparent that, in my desire to create a positive relationship, I had over-promised in terms of fast deliveries and had not then given detailed information to the delivery department. I felt that this alone identified a failure in my consolidation and development approach so I decided to build in a more realistic timescale into my presentation, and also to give improved data to other departments in my company, ensuring that we worked as a team.

Subsequent customer feedback indicated that I was approaching things differently and being realistic about delivery times.

Summary

This chapter is about evaluating your action research. It looks at purposes, positionality and different forms of evaluation. The aim of evaluation is to assess the quality and effectiveness of the research process and the practice it investigates. Establishing criteria therefore becomes a central issue, in order to generate evidence from the data to test the validity of knowledge claims. Evaluation is linked with consolidating and developing, which explores issues about quality of delivery and understanding and developing relationships to ensure a continuing enhancement of customer experience.

Having explored aspects of the sales process, we now consider the significance of your sales research and how it may be made public.

PART III
Significance, Influence and Making Public

An essential part of research is to explain the significance and potential implications of your research and practice. This is the 'making public' phase of a research project. You explain to other people what you have done, why you have done it and why they should take your new knowledge seriously. You disseminate your findings through producing a report that sets out what you have learnt and how you are going to do things differently in future. Your report may take various forms: a standard written report, a website or blog, a company memo or an article to a trade magazine, whatever is appropriate for your needs.

This part contains Chapters 8 and 9.

Chapter 8 gives ideas about the possible significance of researching your sales practice, and how others may benefit from learning about your research. It takes a largely narrative form, to highlight the frequently used narrative form of action research reports.

Chapter 9 sets out how to write a report, according to different conventions and reader expectations. Learning to write and communicate effectively is essential if you wish to reach a wider audience.

Chapter 8

The Significance and Potential Implications of Your Action Research

This chapter is about the significance of your research and some of its potential implications for different people and constituencies. 'Significance' is linked with the idea of 'meaning'. Explaining the significance of your research means you can explain how you have given greater meaning to your work and life and brought visible benefits to yourself and others.

Being able to articulate these ideas is important for when you present your research to colleagues and write up your research report (Chapter 9). Others, including supervisors, managers and colleagues, can learn from you and see how and why they should do their own action research.

Your research is significant for many areas, including the following:

- for yourself;

- for your profession;

- for your organisation;

- for higher education.

There is broad overlap between these areas but organising them like this may help you analyse them for your studies.

As you read this chapter you will see that its form is something like Bakhtin's (1981) idea of heteroglossia, a multiplicity of voices from different perspectives that come together through language to form a unity. This is appropriate for action research, which always has a narrative form, and where stories contain multiple voices.

Here is a story you may find interesting. It contains a main story, about developing communities of educational enquiry, and this contains embedded stories by four action researchers. One, John, works in further education and writes the backstory. The others – Anna, Jan and Julian – are from different backgrounds and settings, and each writes one of the three stories below.

The various stories are interspersed with the voices of the authors of the book, who link ideas with related conceptual frameworks.

Main Story: Developing Communities of Educational Enquiry

BACKSTORY: JOHN'S STORY

My name is John and I am a lecturer in the UK further education sector. I have been doing action research for some years and encourage people who come on courses to explore it for their continuing professional education. Following the lead of prominent international action researchers like Margaret Riel[1] and Bob Dick.[2] I also have a website where I post resources and practitioners' accounts. I also run a regular blog. I get a lot of enquiries from practitioners working in all kinds of professions, and some send in their accounts of practice, often through the blog. Three of these stories, received during the past two years, have had great significance for me, because I am scheduled to take on a new responsibility. My institution has asked me effectively to act as sales consultant to promote their higher degree programmes in the Middle East and to recruit students to those programmes. I am beginning to develop my understanding of sales, and what I know I have learned from stories like the following. I have also learned ways in which the individual stories are significant in themselves, and their collective significance for sales and salespeople (of whom I shall soon be one).

Story 1: Anna's story: The significance of my action research for myself

My name is Anna. I am 58 years old and a former primary school teacher. I took voluntary redundancy three years ago because of school re-organisation. At about the same time I became widowed after a happy marriage of 26 years. The experience was deeply traumatic, with a sense that life has lost a good deal of its meaning. However,

---

1   http://ccar.wikispaces.com/AR+Tutorial.
2   http://scu-au.academia.edu/BobDick.

I forced myself to recover and cope, so, because I believe in making the best of things, I decided to take up interests I had long wished to pursue. These were studying and writing.

My writing took the form of stories with progressive themes for pre-school children. I enjoyed writing the stories and illustrating them. They contained little questions to encourage children to think. They also contained funny surprises to keep the children on their toes. Doing this satisfied my value of contributing to our greatest resource – open, enquiring young minds. To my delight, writing and the studies I later embarked on helped me do much the same. In fact, it became highly significant for my personal life and what began to emerge as a workplace practice.

An important conceptual framework is re-thinking your identity. When you undertake action research you often transform your identity from practitioner to researcher. You learn to speak with a researcher voice; you become fluent in offering analyses, descriptions and explanations of practice. You speak with the authority and wisdom of experience. Critically evaluating practices comes more easily: you think of conceptual frameworks to help make sense of practice.

I investigated how I could get my books printed and distributed. It was not difficult given that many printers now print books on demand, for reasonable prices, and I was then able to distribute them to friends and colleagues in schools I knew. The books proved quite popular: it was never going to be a business with massive turnovers, but sufficient to keep me occupied and earn a small income.

I became interested in the whole field of writing, publishing and selling, so decided to study it more seriously. The only course I could find that would accommodate my interests was an MBA course at a university about 100 miles away. I was accepted on the basis of my experience and existing professional qualifications. It was interesting to be studying again with younger people, some half my age, yet we all shared an enjoyment of learning.

Part of the course involved doing a research project, and I chose to use an action research methodology, which I was already vaguely familiar with from my continuing professional development (CPD) experience at school. Getting deeply involved now proved to be a life-changing experience, because a new field opened up in front of me. I felt, for the first time in my life, that I was doing proper research into my new and unexpected practice of being an author, publisher and bookseller. Part of our studies was of course reading, and I was delighted to find new authors who spoke to my interests of moving from practitioner to researcher. I was thrilled to read Sennett's (2008) ideas about transforming from apprenticeship to craftsperson, and Lave and Wenger's (1991) ideas about moving from the periphery to take one's rightful place as an insider among equals. Mezirow's (2009, 2000) ideas about transformational learning were exciting, and helped me make sense of my rapidly changing self-identification. I loved a book by Antjie Krog (2003) who describes how people changed their identities in post-apartheid South Africa (it brought back memories of a holiday we had taken in Cape Town some years ago). Ideas from Handy and Handy (2002) about the possibilities of creating a whole new life after the age of 60 gave me hope. I loved the realisation that I did not have to remain stuck in the persona I had occupied for many years.

This idea of changing one's identity is an important and liberating concept for many reasons, including the following:

- The idea of 'identity' is often seen as stable and unshifting for the duration of our lives. This is simply not the case. We change by the moment, according to what we hear and experience through our relationships with others and the culture. Think of the different identities you assume when speaking with a close friend in a pub, a customer and a manager in an office. We become shape-shifters according to the company we are in. Identity is not a stable phenomenon. It is a cloak we put on and a language we speak in our practices.

- Many people allocate 'identities' to people in terms of one single category. Sen (2007) produces a wonderful critique when speaking about how religion is often used as this kind of single characterisation: we tend to identify ourselves as Muslims, or Christians, or Hindus, not as taxpayers, animal rights activists or music lovers. Currently you may believe you occupy the single identity of 'only a salesperson', but perhaps not that of a professional, an academic and an author. People have dozens of identities every moment and can easily live them all simultaneously if they wish. Do you want to be all the persons you can be or remain constrained by how other people identify you?

My course requirements included doing a project, which needed to be practice-based. The practice I had now was writing, publishing and bookselling, so I decided to research this. I felt comfortable calling myself a writer and even a publisher, but not a salesperson. I would never have identified myself like this, possibly because of my preconceptions about glib, fast-talking extroverts. Whilst interacting with the literatures of sales, I could not relate to those which promoted a martial approach with words like 'hard-hitting, dogged, first place or no place'. However, I learned that instead of accepting those traditional attitudes of sales, I could develop the different abilities required to sell and adapt them to my existing strengths. I not only changed my identity, but also came to new understandings about what changing one's identity involves.

Identity is often confused with the scripts we speak. Questions arise about which script you speak and who writes it. Do you speak a populist script of salespeople as always looking for others' vulnerabilities in order to deceive them? Or do you speak your own script of caring for others and wishing to do the best you can by them? Either way carries consequences for how others see you and relate to you. You need to be aware and choose what is best according to what you believe in.

When you investigate your practice as a salesperson, you use your talents. You are, in Arendt's (1958) terms, realising your natality: you bring something new to the world in yourself and your work; you occupy your given place well, and use it wisely. In her (1967) book *Men in Dark Times*, Arendt also explains how particular enlightened people brought light to the negative turbulences of the early twentieth century. You can fulfil a similar role in this early twenty-first century. The times are full of turbulence, with massive social, political and economic disruptions. You can bring the voice of sanity to the economic and financial world by showing how it is possible to create dialogical relationships in a context that is pivotal to the world of business. You can influence ideas about how to avoid and overcome the cultures of alienation spoken about in Chapter 1, and encourage social cohesion.

I have especially enjoyed the work of Noam Chomsky (1986) who appears to say that each person is born with the capacity for unlimited creativity in language. I like McNiff's (2002, 2013a) adaptation of Chomsky's ideas, maintaining we are each born with the capacity for an unlimited number of original acts. If we are born to action, as Arendt says, we can act in original creative ways to influence the quality of others' lives as well as our own, including our customers and colleagues. We are not passive bystanders but intentional political actors. We become activists; we think for ourselves; we resist the imposition of ideas by powerful voices that tell us to create ourselves in their image, and instead create ourselves as we wish to be. Judyth Sachs (2003) speaks about teachers as activists who influence processes of organisational change: I am still a teacher and have also become an activist salesperson capable of influencing organisational and cultural change, beginning with myself. We can all make ourselves critical; we can look behind the spoken words and read the sub-text to reveal the insidious voices of propaganda and media spin. We can inspire ourselves to read scholarly books. This is what I have done.

Doing your research has enabled you to speak for yourself. Foucault (2001) speaks of *parrhesia*, the need and responsibility for each person to tell the truth as they see it. You can engage in debates about the principles and practices of sales with authority However, exercising *parrhesia* carries risks and consequences: it can be dangerous to speak truth in organisations because this usually means speaking truth to power. Alford (2001) outlines some of the risks: you are put in an office down the corridor so it is difficult to meet with others, or you are not put on mailing lists. You are made invisible.

Learning about the concept of parrhesia and linking it to the idea of critique has helped my sales confidence. In the past, I would have accepted other people's opinions for a quiet life. I now find that I am prepared to try and influence other people's thinking. This has meant being prepared respectfully to interrogate their beliefs and introduce other approaches. This has usually led to shared agreement and progress in the sales process.

It is important to speak for oneself. Marx made the point (2013) that the question is whether people can represent themselves or need to be represented. From experience I know that the dominant organisational and corporate orthodoxy is that people should not speak for themselves (Chomsky 2000). Challenging organisational power can be problematic yet it is the basis of new practices, and I have found how to do this without incurring the wrath of others because of my new-found knowledge of the art of selling. I have found how to sell ideas, both through my books and through my practice as a salesperson. I have learned how to influence, once again through teaching; I have taken control of my own learning and practice. I like to think I have become an extended professional and can explain what I am doing; and I hope to get advanced certification to show this to be the case. I have made myself powerful, in the sense that I speak with academic authority. I have earned this.

These ideas have implications for how you can contribute to the evolution of your profession.

Story 2: Jan's story: The significance of my research for my profession

My name is Jan and I am from Holland. I have recently started working in a travel agency where I sell personalised tours to overseas visitors. My work depends largely on my good communication skills, both in spoken and written language. For example, I make a lot of telephone contacts, produce copy for the company website and brochures, and conduct guided tours. Also, much of what I say and write is in English. So, to improve my language and sales capacity I recently attended a course on writing and communication run by our local college. They had a strong commitment to action research, so I learned the value of using this as a methodology. I also registered for an English language course to make sure my English stayed up to standard. My studies were funded by my organisation, and my employer was especially pleased at the action research orientation, since she had studied for her MA in management using an action research approach.

The courses were useful, especially the action research aspect, which led me to develop my competence and capacity as a salesperson. When I updated my employer on my progress, she suggested I could use my learning to help work colleagues to do the same. I did so, and found that I was helping them build confidence to give action research a try. They often asked for advice about how to research a particular element of their practices. They were learning with and from me and I was learning with and from them. It was a real collaborative learning experience.

My manager became involved in the work, which strengthened the collaborative ethic. She wanted to develop the idea of evidence-based professionalism for the company. She knew about different forms of knowledge (know that, know how, personal knowledge) and how a body of evidence would count towards understanding sales practices as a form of extended professionalism (Hoyle 1975). She understood the need for different standards of judgement in producing evidence: both the standards of generating facts and figures, and also new dynamic transformational standards to improve the quality of living and customer relations.

The evidence base she, colleagues and I began to develop together provided the basis of the workplace-based reports that we needed to produce for our monthly staff meetings. We were proud to include evidence of our own professionalism in our company literature and for our website. We felt that our promotional literatures were contributing to a new professional literature, a new knowledge base for sales that is written by practitioners for practitioners. Our sales process would become a form of inter-professional learning, where personal professional boundaries could be made fluid so we could learn with and from one another. We felt we were legitimating sales in the eyes of all professions and the public, as well as developing new standards about what counts as professionalism. We also felt that we were helping to prevent sales training from being corporatised by companies who, we felt, belong to an 'owners' club' of knowledge of sales, which can impede the flow and sharing of information.

Through your research you show that practitioners can contribute to new thinking and practices. Especially you can challenge dominant technical forms of discourse that are required by many established professional development courses and academic journals. The fact that this form is accepted reinforces its legitimacy. Foucault describes this phenomenon as a 'regime of truth'. In his

Power/Knowledge (Foucault, 1980) he says that truth is 'linked in circular relation with systems of power which produce and sustain it' (p. 133). He continues:

> *Truth is a thing of this world: it is produced only by virtue of multiple forms of constraint. And it induces regular effects of power. Each society has its regime of truth, its 'general politics' of truth: that is, the types of discourse which it accepts and makes function as true. The mechanisms and instances which enable one to distinguish true and false statements, the means by which each is sanctioned; the techniques and procedures accorded value in the acquisition of truth; and the status of those who are charged with saying what counts as true (Foucault 1980: 130–31).*

Through doing your research you have challenged the existing regime of truth and introduced a new one. You have both raised the status of sales in the practical world, and transformed the hegemony of abstract propositional theory into a form of methodological and epistemological power sharing, where practitioners' practical theories are seen as equally valid and significant.

You have also challenged the idea of surveillance, showing that sales practitioners can regulate their own practices through ongoing self-evaluation. Bourdieu (1990) explains how organisations often put in place systems of surveillance to monitor what employees are doing. He uses the idea of the panopticon, a prison built in a circular form with individual cells facing inwards and the jailor at the centre. This means that prisoners cannot see their neighbours or the jailor, but the jailor can see everyone, and they do not know when the jailor is watching. It also means that the jailor can disappear but no one knows. The prisoners end up monitoring themselves, and over time this becomes an accepted form of life, an Orwellian society of Big Brother who is never seen yet who exists in the psyche of citizens. It is the current image of corporate bureaucratic control, where financial and industrial elites maintain control of the media so that social patterns are firmly established in the public mind and become embedded in the culture (Swartz 1997). By becoming a self-actuated practitioner, unconstrained by others' surveillance and oriented towards growth and achievement, you demonstrate the benefits of your study to your sales practices and so contribute to the development of your profession.

On reflection, I think I have become a change agent, and I have thought seriously about what this means. Many literatures seem to assume that a change agent changes other people. I am not sure it is possible to 'change' people in ways that can lead to the kind of sustainable, independent thinking appropriate for professional development.

This would mean their criticality is lost. Professional education is not about turning out robots; it is about encouraging people's originality of mind.

I see my responsibility, as a sales professional, to help colleagues to think critically. When I offer them my services, I remember that they are not simply accepting everything I say. They are filtering it through their capacity for criticality. They ask themselves, 'Should I believe what Jan is saying? Are his ideas well grounded?' I deliberately encourage debates about our interactions, to help them see that what they are experiencing is also what they do with clients, such as when they engage in manipulative behaviour, and the need to be honest and open about some of the limitations of our services while also pointing out the benefits.

I hope I am encouraging new attitudes towards the concepts of change agency and professional development. I emphasise consistently that I have influenced my own processes of change, and am encouraging others to do the same. Rather than anticipating that people can be changed, I think instead of how I can exercise my educational influence in people's thinking so that they think for themselves. I am always ready and willing to help them learn how to do things themselves.

This idea of becoming a change agent is important from the perspective of Senge's ideas about what it takes for an organisation to become a learning organisation (1990: 6–9). He speaks of the five disciplines necessary for transforming an organisation into a learning organisation. These are:

1. Systems thinking, where everything is understood as connected with everything else. People, ideas, actions and contexts are all interlinked. This is the most important discipline according to Senge, and includes the following four disciplines.

2. Personal mastery, which refers to our capacity to refine ideas, re-think and re-organise.

3. Mental models: this emphasises that personal control involves self-critique and being able to question one's own taken-for-granted assumptions.

4. Building shared vision: we need a sense of where we are going in order to help us get there. Clearly identified outcomes are not necessary, so much as working towards a better situation than at present.

5.   Team learning: We can often learn from and with others more effectively than when we learn by ourselves. Critical feedback and dialogue are essential.

It must always be remembered that embarking on any path of personal growth is a matter of choice. Forcing someone to do something is guaranteed to backfire, and organisations can get into considerable difficulty if they become too aggressive in promoting ideas about personal development.

I have benefited from learning specific content matters, but have perhaps benefited even more by appreciating the need for sustained personal critique. It is essential for all participants in an organisation to see themselves as thinking agents, not simply as people who do as they are told. I try to encourage all to think and speak for themselves, and I create opportunities, such as sales team meetings, to develop a culture of dialogue and shared experience.

Now let's look at the significance of your research for the development of your organisation, especially in terms of how it could become a learning organisation.

Story 3: Julian's story: The significance of my research for my company

I am Julian, a former instructor in Physical Education. I work for a company that provides activity and skills development classes to schools and clubs, especially in areas of low economic status and often in conditions of real need. In the past two years we have worked with several schools and evening youth clubs, where we have sold our fitness and skills development programmes at accessible prices. This has been successful and has rolled out well among this group. There has been a huge demand for the service, which has been good news for our company.

A problem developed, however. This was an issue of cash flow. The training had to be conducted as an after school or evening activity, as obviously pupils would be attending school during the day. Therefore we had to bring in more staff to provide the programmes and pay them higher wages than normal for unsocial hours. We wanted to keep our prices low because we were providing a service that was educational in itself, and mainly for underprivileged children, so this made us think creatively about how to solve the problem.

During previous study for a bachelor's degree in sports science I had encountered the idea of action research. I decided to use this to explore areas not previously seen as target areas. It occurred to me that we could make our programmes available to groups we had not considered before. I approached the company with the suggestion and was asked to do a presentation to the board. My suggestion was that we could provide the same fitness and skills development programmes to retired people, tailored to their specific needs. This had several advantages. We could sell the programmes at a higher price and employ our staff at times of the day they had not previously been able to work, because our new client group, unlike the children, could attend during the day. This also would smooth our cash flow as it would bring in a greater continuous income. The board was interested and gave me the task of investigating the area and finding new prospects and markets for development.

We explored the idea, using an action research approach to prospecting, connecting and appointing, and drawing up strategic action plans. We succeeded in delivering programmes to six adult day classes, where mature people began to enjoy relaxed but organised skills programmes including ball games, modified yoga exercises and breathing and healthy sleep training. There was an enormous demand for our services, both from the schools and now the retirement sector. We have taken on staff to meet the demand.

I am developing new thinking and am being asked to take on new organisational responsibilities. I like to theorise my practices in terms of what I learned from my undergraduate studies. I can see that I am contributing to developing my organisation as a 'learning organisation', and that this involves several strands working side-by-side: (1) organisational learning, which refers to the strategies and processes involved to support individual and collective learning within an organisation, and (2) the learning organisation, which aims to evaluate and promote learning processes in organisations (Easterby-Smith et al. 1999; Tsang 2013). I am also familiar with more recent ideas about the knowledge-creating company (Nonaka and Takeuchi 1995), and even the knowledge-creating society (Hargreaves 2003; UNESCO reports, including 2013). It is interesting to reflect that all these ideas are linked with knowledge and theories of different kinds. They emphasise the idea that what we know influences what we do, so what we do can be enhanced by continuing learning. I can see that this idea is particularly useful in sales where each encounter provides the opportunity to learn and in turn apply this learning to one's sales practice.

I have especially enjoyed reading the work of Argyris and Schön. Throughout they argue that change is a stable phenomenon of social living (see Schön's 1973). I enjoyed ideas, influenced by Argyris's earlier work (for example, his 1964), about theories of action. The generic term 'theories of action' include two kinds of theories: 'theories-in-use' and 'espoused theories'. Theories-in-use are the theories we use to guide our everyday lives: for example, we may choose to drive to work or walk, depending on our commitments, perhaps whether we wish to get to work early, or avoid extra fuel emissions.

Espoused theories form the basis of what we say to other people (and often to ourselves): for example, a person may say, 'I drove to work this morning because I wanted to get here early to complete my report', but the reality may have been that they were feeling too tired to walk or it was raining. The point made by Argyris and Schön is that theories-in-use tend to be tacit: we are unaware of what we are thinking and don't stop to reflect on whether we are thinking our own thoughts or what other people have taught us to think, whereas espoused theories are our conscious aspirations: what we would like to be the case. We need to become aware of the potential contradictions and try to make the two sets of theories congruent.

I could see that these ideas linked with Argyris and Schön's ideas about single loop, double loop and triple loop learning (page 62 of this book). The idea of triple loop learning was especially significant for me because colleagues and I were learning from our experience and using our new learning for new circumstances.

Argyris and Schön elaborated on single, double and triple loop learning with ideas about what they call Model I and Model II practices. In Model I practices, people tend to use theories-in-use; they go on often unwarranted assumptions about other people and practices as well as themselves ('She is not very friendly; I can't do it; I am not clever enough'). Such assumptions can be major inhibitors to personal, social and organisational growth because people are held back by prejudices and anxieties. A major emphasis in organisational learning is to help people find ways to overcome these internalised mental habits by seeing them for what they are. People become more reflective about the ways they think, and begin to see that they are holding themselves back by established, but possibly damaging, ways of thinking. This can move people into what Argyris and Schön call Model II practices, where they become more open to new ways of thinking and acting, without the deadweight of their own prejudgements.

These ideas link with those of Kahneman (2011), especially about System 1 and System 2 thinking (see page 135). System 1 thinking is the kind that immediately looks for ready associations and is rapid and unreflective. For example, when we hear the terms 'taxi driver' or 'doctor' we tend to associate these with males (at least in most western societies), whereas 'nurse' or 'teacher' are frequently associated with a female. We learn cultural norms and anticipate them to be the case. In System 2 thinking we stop and interrogate what we are saying, and how this may be informed by earlier experiences or learned habits of mind.

Kahneman spoke about the need to re-frame issues and the kind of choices people make when they stop and think about what they are thinking. Schön also went on to develop ideas about framing and reframing for different contexts: see his and Rein's (1994) *Frame Reflection*, where they explain how organisational support strategies can help people develop more open ways of thinking. They bring this idea to the field of intractable policy controversies, and argue that before people can begin to talk about engaging with and possibly resolving intractable situations they first have to interrogate their own habits of mind and internalised prejudices.

This idea is important for sales practices. In situations where you as a salesperson may have difficulty in making calls, or experience a drop in self-esteem when a deal falls through, it is important to remember that each encounter brings new opportunities for success. Many people get bogged down in remembered bad times: they forget they are agents who can create new good times, and can re-create themselves as they wish to be. This can be liberating for salespeople who think they need to live up to stereotypical brash approaches or get discouraged through lack of immediate success or possible negative feedback from customers. You can change this. There is nothing to stop you except perhaps your own anxiety that stops you trying. It does take courage and some positive self-talk, but it can be done, and doing your action research can be a strong vehicle for helping the process along. In this sense, action research can be seen as a core strategy for organisational learning. Because you have succeeded in pursuing an action enquiry, and can produce the evidence in the form of your report, you qualify yourself as a person whose opinion is to be trusted and taken seriously. You can set precedents for the future direction and character of your own organisation, especially in terms of collaborative learning. A learning organisation is not a thing to be aimed for but actually comes into being through the practice.

However, this point calls for some critique.

There is an undercurrent theme in the business and sales management literatures that scientific management (Taylorism) has never gone away. There is still an assumption that roles are organised hierarchically, reinforced by a general understanding that only technical, linear and outcomes-based knowledge is valid and that only certain people may be classified as knowers and theorists. Delves Broughton's (2009) *What They Teach You at Harvard Business School* is a reasonably accurate caricature of this view. There is still a dominant assumption that business schools should train business people to learn about the theory of business and also learn an equally important (though unspoken) message about who should own the theory.

These ideas can be seen in workplaces everywhere and raises questions about whether salespeople would be allowed to change their identities and exercise their originality of mind. Labour is still hierarchically organised. While valued forms of knowledge may be changing from excellence in skills and competencies to excellence in web-based technology and knowledge creation, the issue of who produces and uses knowledge has not. When Schön speaks about 'shared vision', whose vision is it, and does everyone want to share it? Do we want to be part of a team (Schrage 1990), and if so, who decides the team's membership?

I have become aware of how I am caught up in the struggle for the democratisation of knowledge. Especially I have become aware of how I can influence matters by promoting the idea of action research. I am contributing to a culture that values all participants' contributions to knowledge. This has been done in other professions so why not in sales? I encourage others not to be content with consuming knowledge but to create it, and influence processes of change through engaging in those processes. Working with colleagues, I believe I am influencing my organisation to become a learning organisation. It may take a long time and involve one step at a time, but I have begun the process, and hope that others can learn with and from me.

I am beginning to develop new organisational practices to encourage colleagues to engage in their workplace studies, with a view to getting higher degree accreditation from the university I graduated from. Working with the university, and with senior organisational management, I am initiating a pilot programme of sales training, using an action research approach. This is structured as a semester-long module for a masters programme, comprising three weekend meetings with online and in-house support provided by myself between meetings. Part of the programme is a requirement to undertake an action enquiry into some element of their sales practice. I am negotiating for some remission of time for colleagues who wish to participate, though probably the first cohort will need to complete the module to convince senior management that the initiative is worthwhile. Senior management have already committed to purchasing the services of a professional developer from the university, which is a most progressive step and a demonstration of their commitments to organisational professional learning. Acceptance on the programme carries some obligations: participants must commit to full attendance at the three meetings, to complete required pre-meeting readings and to write a post-programme report about what they have learned from the experience. We hope to produce an in-house bulletin of the initiative, for distribution to the entire workforce. This, we hope, will encourage all to be interested in developing their own practices, and to seeing the value of doing so for themselves and for the organisation.

BACKSTORY: JOHN'S STORY: THE SIGNIFICANCE OF MY RESEARCH FOR HIGHER EDUCATION

John now continues the wider story.

My aim in developing the website and writing a blog is to encourage salespeople to post their stories of professional learning so other salespeople can learn and develop their thinking. I am also encouraging my colleagues in the college to explore their identities and practices as salespeople. I hope that this strategy will encourage new self-perceptions by academics and salespersons to see themselves as crossing boundaries into one another's domains and taking on one another's identities. The stories from Anna, Jan and Julian will contribute to this new knowledge base, and so will mine. I hope this public knowledge base will help salespeople to develop confidence in their professionalism, and influence public perceptions about what it means to be a salesperson.

It is widely acknowledged that higher education is changing in many ways. The very concept of 'the university' is in question and universities are themselves caught up in a culture of corporatisation. They are identified by their brands; academics are required to teach programmes that will 'produce' 'knowledge workers'. Universities are subjected to increasing governance through the technologies of performativity (Lyotard 1984: 46) by corporate watchdogs. Moves are afoot to privatise them even more by introducing new 'captains of industry' in the form of vice chancellors drawn from the business world 'At the macro level ... performativity is about securing the best possible contribution of higher education to the best possible performance of the socio-economic system' says Fanghanel (2012: 18). The ethos of higher education has changed significantly with the new neoliberal rush for market domination, where knowledge becomes a commodity to be bought and sold for profit: practices are 'both academic and economic in order to account for the turning of higher education into a service and of the service into knowledge loaded trade' (Vlăsceanu 2010: 20). While there is a vigorous critique in the literatures asking what universities are for (Collini 2012), it has little influence on corporate thinking: the machinery of globalisation churns away, a new 'modern times' except that the efficiency of industrialisation has been replaced by the efficiency of technologised knowledge management.

Academics are caught up in this situation. They are positioned as salespeople in an increasingly competitive market, especially when prospecting for overseas students or when establishing off-campus sites, as, for example, in Education City in Doha, Qatar. Yet most academics strongly resist the idea that this is how they should be seen. While they accept that they must teach curricula that are designed with market interests in mind, they do not accept that they are 'selling' programmes (or ideas, for that matter). There is enormous reluctance, especially in those universities designated as elite institutions, to change the self-image from working with ideas to working in the marketplace. The reason for this could be that academics still see sales according to the dominant discourses and images of salespeople, failing to recognise that new sales practices are developing in sales, as outlined in this book, or that new forms of theory are accepted in universities, which allow practitioners to see themselves as researchers and theorists. But where is the public literature celebrating salespeople's stories and accounts of learning?

From the messages communicated in this book perhaps sales needs to come into the broader field of educational research, because the work of salespeople, as we hope has become evident, is a form of teaching and learning. They teach themselves and their customers to make wise choices, and both parties learn from the other in the process. The best teachers are those who see themselves as learners, and if learning is about finding something out, then it is equally a form of research. Sales research becomes educational research.

This understanding may greatly help academics who can, to a certain extent, still create their own roles and can definitely create their own self-perceptions. If they are positioned as salespeople, at least they can learn from on-the-job salespeople about how to sell properly. This calls for a dual approach. On the one hand, academics need to develop their understandings of new attitudes and approaches to sales – this calls for new professional education programmes for academics; on the other hand, salespeople need to be more prepared to study their practices and place their scholarly accounts of practice in the public domain. To do this, academics need to create programmes for salespeople to study their practices towards masters and doctoral accreditation, and do so themselves, collaboratively with those whose studies they support.

This view does not at all diminish the idea of the university. On the contrary, it strengthens it, for universities are not buildings but comprise real people, working collaboratively to produce knowledge that will benefit all. Nussbaum (1997) celebrates this idea; drawing on the ideas of Seneca, she writes:

> *An education is truly 'fitted for freedom' only if it is such as to **produce** free citizens, citizens who are free not because of wealth or birth, but because they can call their minds their own. Male and female, slave-born and freeborn, rich and poor, they have looked into themselves and*

developed the ability to separate mere habit and convention from what
they can defend by argument. They have ownership of their own thought
and speech, and this imparts to them a dignity that is far beyond the
outer dignity of class and rank (p. 293; emphasis in original).

But this will happen only if and when academics and salespeople decide to close the gap that divides them, as noted in Chapter 1. It will happen only when academics and salespeople interrogate established ideas about what counts as knowledge and who counts as a knower; and acknowledge that, while this kind of development requires a systemic view, they fully engage with the idea that systems begin with individuals. This would mean a new interpretation of Drucker's (1967) original idea of the knowledge economy as social interchange, where we all learn together and benefit from the experience, where the currency relates to the wealth of people, their happiness, which money cannot buy.

Summary

This chapter considers the significance of your action research in sales and why people should take it seriously. Issues arising include the capacity of individuals to create their identities according to their own values system; the right and responsibility to speak their truth as they see it; and the responsibility to exercise agency in processes of personal and social change. We look at the importance of your research for yourself, your profession, your organisation and for higher education. It is suggested that practitioner-based sales research has much to offer across a range of areas, including the academy. Articulating the significance of your research is a core element of making it public, which is the focus of Chapter 9.

Chapter 9

Writing Your Action Research Report

Whether you are on a professional development course or a degree programme, you will need to write a report. This may take a variety of forms: possibly a report for your company, a module on a university course or a dissertation. Whatever form it takes, you need to know some basic principles, both about what the report will look like, how to write it and how it will be judged. You also need to be confident about its potential for influence in the public domain.

This chapter deals with these issues and is organised as follows:

- What writing any report involves.

- Developing your writing skills.

- What writing an action research report involves.

- How your report will be judged.

- The potential influence of your writing.

Our advice throughout is to approach the job of writing in the same way as you approach the job of selling: the knowledge and skills required for both practices are similar. When you sell any product or service you develop:

- your product and service knowledge;

- your knowledge of the procedures of selling;

- knowledge of your customer;

- knowledge of competitors.

When you write for a reader you do the same. Writing is both product and process: you write as a practice to produce a piece of writing as a product. Good writing involves understanding the concept of AIDA (attention, interest, desire and action). In writing you sell ideas, so the knowledge you develop becomes:

- knowledge of writing about your practice (knowledge of selling and what it involves);

- knowledge of how to write and organise ideas (knowing what makes a good text and how to maintain your reader's attention);

- knowledge of how to write for an identified reader (knowing who your reader is, and writing for their needs);

- knowledge of other competitors in the field (knowing who else is working with the same ideas and how you can produce a text that will position you at the forefront of your field).

It can be useful to approach the job of writing as a research project, in the same way as you have researched your practice of selling. You ask critical questions about what you need to investigate, why you need to investigate it, how you can monitor and keep records of what you are doing, and how to ask advice from others. McNiff has written elsewhere about how to research your writing practice (McNiff forthcoming, 2014); here we offer some practical advice about writing an action research report for sales, including how to write, what it involves and how your writing will be used.

What Writing Any Report Involves

As with any practice, some people seem to have a natural talent for writing while others have to struggle. One thing is sure: all writers have to work at their craft. Good writing takes a small amount of talent and a lot of hard work. It also takes a lot of time. This means you have to be prepared to put in effort and organise your life to accommodate your writing practice. It also means being prepared to spend time working alone. Writing requires focus, and sometimes this can be achieved only in complete, or near complete, solitude, or at least with minimal distraction. Having said this, ignore advice that says you have to sit facing the wall, and for only certain periods of time during the day. As long as you get on with it, you can work out your own schedule and way of working.

GETTING STARTED

Producing a good piece of writing means asking practical questions about your reasons and purposes for producing your text. As a vital first step, think about your anticipated audience and ask yourself the questions below, and write down ideas in a notebook as they occur to you (if you write down your ideas on the spot you may find you have a working draft for a more extended text).

- Who am I writing this report for?

- Why am I writing it?

- What do I wish to say? What is special about what I wish to say? In what way is it original?

- What else do I hope to communicate?

- What form will my report take?

Who am I writing this report for?

Think about whom you are writing for, and develop a sense of audience. Write in a way that your reader will expect and appreciate. If this is a workplace report, write so that your company manager or colleagues will understand what you are saying. If you are writing a module assignment or a dissertation, write in a more scholarly style that your supervisor or examiner will accept. Keep focused on the person you have identified as your reader and write for them.

Why am I writing it?

You are writing to let your reader know about what you have done in your action research, so write with a sense of purpose. Your reader does not know what you have done or anything about you. All they know is what they read on the page, so it is your responsibility to tell them what they need to know. Tell them who you are, where you work, what you have done in your action research, why you have done it and what you have achieved. Also tell them why it is important that they should read what you are writing. You need to take your work seriously so that other people will do so too.

What do I wish to say? What is special about what I wish to say? In what way is it original?

Tell your reader about your action research and why you are excited about it. What have you done that no one else has done? What is your claim to knowledge? Tell your reader what you know now that you did not know before, and in what way it is special, whether for yourself or for other people, and possibly what other people can learn from you. Be clear about what you wish to say, and stick to the point. If you think you have improved your selling techniques, say what you have done and what it has involved. If you think you have become more reflective, explain to your reader what this means for you and others, and how you have done it.

What else do I hope to communicate?

Aim to communicate what you have learned and how you have learned it. You may wish to explain that you have improved your communication and selling skills and are demonstrating this now through your writing. You have also developed your capacities for lifelong learning and for reflective practice and are using these for your own and others' benefit. Your current writing acts as evidence. Think of the most significant aspects of what doing your action research means for you and others, and let your reader know.

What form will my report take?

Write your report as a story. Story is now used everywhere in professional education contexts (Moon 2010). You are not writing a descriptive story, though: it is an explanatory story, an account of your action enquiry. Aim to show its cyclical form, from identifying an initial research issue and question at the beginning of your project to making your knowledge claim at the end. This involves describing and explaining how you moved forward through asking critical questions; how you worked collaboratively with others and listened to their advice; how you gathered data and generated evidence in relation to specifically articulated criteria and standards, and so on. Use a narrative form, that is, tell the story of what you did, making sure you offer descriptions (what you did), explanations (why you did it and what you hoped to achieve), and reflections (what you learned from the experience). Make sure, too, that you observe the need for rhetoric, that is, you tell your reader what you are going to say, explain what you are saying as you say it, and summarise what you have said when you have said it.

Developing Your Writing Skills

We said above that good writing involves a small amount of talent and a lot of hard work. This is the case for even the most successful writers. Here are the main points to bear in mind. They are much the same points that you would think about for your sales practice.

WRITING TAKES TIME AND PRACTICE

In the same way as preparing for a business meeting with your customer takes time and practice, so does writing. You must schedule writing into your daily routine. Make it a golden rule that you work on your piece of writing every day, even if it is to read what you wrote yesterday and perhaps add ten words. If you do not stay in touch with your writing you will forget it, and catching up again makes the job twice as long (and seriously frustrating). Do not expect everything to fall into place immediately. Spend time on planning what you are going to say and how you hope to say it. Draw up initial plans and structures and use these as blueprints for the writing task. A useful strategy is to produce a PowerPoint presentation with bullet points for each slide.

DRAFTING

Many people think they can produce a piece of writing in one go. This is seldom the case, even for the most experienced writers. Everyone – everyone – has to produce multiple drafts. The best and most readable texts achieve their quality because authors are prepared to spend large amounts of time on editing and refining. It is rather like comedians: the best and most spontaneous comedians spend hours rehearsing their spontaneity. A final text usually goes through umpteen versions, and often what you end up with is far from what you thought you would write in the beginning. And even then, when you read your final text, you still want to make changes – but you have to submit the manuscript at some point, so produce the best text you can in the time available.

WRITE FOR A READER

Many people make a serious error of writing for themselves rather than a reader. They assume that the reader knows who they are, where they work and what their contexts and situations are. This is not the case. Often your reader knows only your name as it appears on the page: they have no clues about where you work, what the social, political, cultural aspects of your work are, or how you see yourself. You have to tell them these things. As well as writing about substantive issues (that is, what ideas you are communicating), give your reader directions to help them navigate their way through your text. Say things like, 'In this chapter I wish to discuss ...' and '... as I indicated on page 23 ...' and 'This idea links with an idea by Schön (1983) who spoke about ...' Keep your reader on track, and help them to see where they are in your text: it is your responsibility to guide them, not their responsibility to try to work out where they are. Besides, as any salesperson knows, if you don't give your customer clues and maintain momentum, they will lose interest quickly.

DO YOUR MARKET RESEARCH

Do your market research: do your prospecting. Check out what your readers want and make sure you give it to them. Find out which assessment criteria they will use and write so you fulfil these. If you are writing a workplace report for your company manager or colleagues, anticipate what they need to know, and give them the information. Check out the required style of writing, number of words you need to produce, form of referencing and any required structures. Look at successful pieces of writing. If you are writing a dissertation, look in the institutional library; if you are writing a journal article, look at past issues of the journal for ideas about what to write and how to write it. Journal editors will tell you that the most common reason for rejecting an article is because the author has submitted it to the wrong journal. Read the instructions, or the handbook, or any advice offered by experienced others, and abide by it. Then, having done your initial research, go for it, and persevere until you produce a successful text.

STYLE OF LANGUAGE

Aim to write in a way that will help your reader see the point of your text easily and appreciate it as a scholarly document. Do this by:

- Writing in an uncluttered way. This means avoiding repetition, exaggeration and waffling. Cut out every 'very'. Keep it neat and tidy.

- Reference your work correctly and appropriately. Make sure you cite the work of people you refer to and get your references right. If you give a direct quotation, always give the page number. Also note: 'quote' and 'quotation' are different words. A quote is what you get from a builder; a quotation is what you get from a writer.

- Use one idea per sentence. Stick to the point and don't confuse issues and ideas.

- Keep your paragraphs focused and not too long. Aim also to break up your text into sections, with appropriate section headings, so it is easy to read and the messages are clear.

- Learn and speak the language of your target audience. If you are writing for your company, write in a professional language that colleagues will appreciate. If you are writing a scholarly document, write in an academic form of language that your supervisor will appreciate. Always write for your reader, not only for yourself.

STRUCTURE YOUR WRITING

Organise your ideas so your reader can see a clear structure to it. If you look at the contents of any book or text, you will see that it is structured so that you are led through the ideas in a smooth and coherent way. A text should in some sense have a beginning, middle and end, although in an action research text the end would always signal a new beginning. Also, the story need not be linear: it can go in interesting directions, but there is always a visible pathway running through (see the idea of a golden thread on page 42). Use section headings and other signposts to help your reader find their way; different weights of fonts can show which sections are 'A', 'B' and 'C'. Summaries can be useful for keeping your reader on track and consolidating their reading before moving on to the next piece. Aim to introduce and summarise main issues and arguments as you go.

PRODUCE A CLEAN MANUSCRIPT

Producing a clean manuscript that you will be proud of means that your text is error-free and pleasing to the eye by being well laid out on the page or computer screen. Achieving this level of professionalism requires thorough editing and meticulous proofreading. Editing refers to the process of reading your text and ensuring that it is coherent: the ideas hang together, they are in an intelligible sequence, all references are supplied and spellings are checked. Proofreading means you check through for technical accuracy: all words are correctly spelt and grammar and punctuation are accurate. You will probably proofread your entire text at least three times. Find a friend who will also proofread for you (but do not expect them to correct your work: this is your job and your responsibility alone).

MANAGING YOUR SCHEDULE

Set yourself a writing schedule, including targets for production of sections or chapters, and stay with it. Aim to do a piece of writing every day, according to your work schedule. Aim to do at least 100 words per day, and increase this target as appropriate. You would be surprised how much you can write during a coffee break or on a train commute. Heed the advice by Pressfield (2011), to start before you are ready. If you wait until you are ready to write you will wait forever. Make up your mind to do it and do it.

These are some basic commonsense ideas about developing your writing skills and managing the writing process. Here are some of the things that writing an action research report involves.

What Writing an Action Research Report Involves

As noted, you would write a report for a range of contexts, such as a progress report, a professional portfolio, a module assignment or dissertation, or a report for your company. Your work may also require you to write proposals and briefing documents. The readers in each of these contexts may expect different things: the expectations for a progress report written for your manager will be different from those for a module assignment. However, all texts that report on your action research would share common elements: these are developed below.

There are several ways of writing an action research report. Here are two commonly used structures.

STRUCTURE 1: TELLING THE STORY OF YOUR ACTION ENQUIRY

Perhaps the easiest way of writing a report is to tell the story of your action enquiry. You would take the questions that informed your original enquiry, and turn them into the past tense, like this:

- Introduction: Set the scene: say who you are and what you do for a living.

- Describe your contexts.

- What did I want to investigate?

- Why did I need to investigate it?

- How do I show the situation as it was and as it developed?

- What could I do? What did I do?

- How did I generate evidence from the data?

- How did I check whether any conclusions I made were reasonably fair and accurate?

- How do I explain the significance of my action research?

- How have I modified my ideas and practices in light of my evaluation?

Here is an outline of a possible report, using these questions as section headings.

Introduction

Say who you are, where you work, and anything specific about yourself that your reader needs to know.

> *My name is John and I am the senior partner in a small two-person estate agency. We live and work in a small, rather sleepy village in Dorset. We have built up our business from scratch and, as well as selling properties, we aim to offer a personalised service to a local clientele. Offering a personalised service and a good customer experience are the core values of our business. We rely a lot on client recommendations to keep our business going. Otherwise our only form of advertising is in the local newspaper. This seems to have served us well so far and we do sufficient business to keep us ticking over.*

Describe your contexts

Give any relevant information about contexts that may help your reader appreciate the reasons and purposes of your enquiry.

> *Our neighbourhood is undergoing refurbishment with funding from local government, and our particular area is receiving some attention. We heard that another more up-market estate agent is about to move*

in, probably because the area promises to be more attractive, and this meant we may face some serious competition.

What did I want to investigate?

Say what your research issue was.

Because of the possible competition, we needed to think seriously about how we could maintain the viability of our business, possibly by improving our service to customers, attracting new clientele and advertising more widely.

Why did I need to investigate it?

Say what was going on that made you want to investigate the situation more deeply. State your research question.

Perhaps it was time for us to expand and think about new ways of marketing and selling our products. This idea of changing our working practices was not comfortable, as we had been doing well so far. However, times change so perhaps it was time for us to do an evaluation of our work and see if it needed improving. Unless we did so we could find ourselves losing customers to the new firm. Our research questions first therefore focused on evaluating our work, and we asked questions such 'How are we doing? Are we doing reasonably well? Can we do things better?'

How did I show the situation as it was and as it developed?

Say how you gathered data to show the situation as it was. Later in your report, say how you gathered data to show the situation as it developed. Say which data-gathering techniques you used to gather your data at different stages of your research. Also say who you identified as your research participants.

After some discussion my partner and I decided that I would take main responsibility for the evaluation, and draw on his experience and knowledge to provide further data. We also decided to ask ten former clients to respond to some questions about how they had experienced our service and whether they had any suggestions about how we could improve it. We drew up a questionnaire and emailed the ten clients to ask them if they would kindly complete it. They agreed so we sent the questionnaire by email. (Attach a blank questionnaire as an appendix to the report.) We assured our clients of complete confidentiality at all times and other ethical aspects.

What could I do? What did I do?

Say what actions you took.

Once we received permission from our ten former clients we distributed the questionnaire. We asked clients to respond by an agreed date. My partner and I also conducted a tape-recorded conversation about how we might develop the agency so that it would appear more upmarket and therefore be a viable competitor for our potential new rivals. We began to imagine ways in which we could improve what we already do, such as updating our website and finding new prospects. While we already had sufficient business to keep us going, we needed to expand our client base just in case our competition proved serious.

How did I generate evidence from the data?

Remember the idea that values can act as criteria to judge the quality of what you are doing. Say how you searched your data to find instances of those values in action. Explain that those pieces of data came to stand as your evidence, to ground your knowledge claims.

I collated the responses from clients. These showed that they appreciated the quality of our service and had found us friendly and helpful. However, some responses indicated areas we could think about improving. These were that we could offer a wider portfolio of houses for purchase, that we could provide more information on our website, and that the actual conveyancing of the property could be handled more effectively. We took these responses seriously, especially as they linked with the conversation between my partner and myself about updating the website and our service in general. This did, however, raise new questions about whether we had the expertise to do these jobs ourselves, or whether we needed to avail of a professional website construction agency. We also wondered about whether we should take on an assistant to help with finding new prospects. Perhaps we should think about developing a proper sales team rather than rely only on our partnership of two? It was difficult for us to change our mindset at this point because we had grown used to working in our small way, but times change.

How did I check that any conclusions I made were reasonably fair and accurate?

Explain how you carried out validity checks to make sure your provisional conclusions were accurate.

> I drew up an informal business development plan and contacted the ten clients who had acted as participants to ask if they would be willing to comment on it. Six said they would, so I sent them the plan (include the plan as Appendix 2 to the report). They sent in varied responses, but all seemed to agree that we needed to modernise in order to stay up to date. I had not anticipated this response, because I had thought the rather old-world nature of our business matched the old-world charm of our village, but evidently not. So reluctantly I accepted that we had to change – or, perhaps more accurately, I needed to change. But at least I was reasonably confident that our core values of good customer experience and personalised service were being realised, and appreciated by all. So, based on these findings, we went ahead and hired a website consultancy firm, and took on an assistant.

How do I explain the significance of my action research?

Explain what the significance of your research is for your own learning and the possible learning of others, and how you are thinking of contributing to new public thinking and practices.

> Our business began to pick up speed. Our new assistant proved a marvellous asset and put a lot of energy into prospecting and appointing. She suggested we offer various perks such as a lower commission fee for the first ten clients who contacted us by a certain date. These changes would not have happened without our conducting our informal evaluation, or without the threat of competition. Perhaps a main lesson is not to wait for threats to appear, but to evaluate what is happening as a regular feature of good professional practice.

How have I modified my ideas and practices in light of my evaluation?

Explain how your research is influencing the development of new thinking and new practices for yourself and others.

We have been approached by the local newspaper who wish to write up our success story. As part of the story we will emphasise the importance of ongoing evaluation, and the need to be open to new ideas and to stay up to date with contemporary thinking and practices. We hope our story will benefit others who may find themselves in a similar situation and help them ensure that their businesses remain viable no matter what the competition.

As an afterword, the anticipated competing estate agency did not move into the area after all. This does not prevent us feeling proud of what we have done, and making sure we keep up to date in future.

STRUCTURE 2: WRITING AN ACADEMIC REPORT

Now imagine that you are writing the same story as an academic report. If you wish, you can keep the same structure as above. The difference for an academic report is that you would engage more thoroughly with the scholarly literatures, and expand arguments and issues. How to do this is outlined below, now using different section headings (which actually say much the same as in Structure 1).

The headings often recommended for writing scholarly reports, including dissertations, theses and journal articles, are as follows:

- aims

- theoretical frameworks

- methodology or modes of enquiry

- data sources and evidence

- findings and/or conclusions

- discussion

- significance.

Broadly speaking, the headings can be interpreted as follows.

Aims

Say what the research is about, why you have undertaken it, and what you hoped to achieve. Give a clear research question, such as 'How do I improve my sales practices?' Always check that you give the reasons and purposes of your research and not only descriptions. If you give only descriptions this makes your work action learning but not necessarily action research.

Theoretical frameworks

This refers to the ideas related to your field of enquiry, and the main authors who publish these ideas. Connecting and appointing could relate to qualities of tenacity (for example, Crawshaw and Jackson, 2010; Freire, 1996), building relationships (for example, Archer and Cameron, 2012) and making dynamic connections (for example, Robinson, 2011).

Methodology or modes of enquiry

A methodology is how you do things: you can use an ethnographic methodology, an action research methodology, an empirical methodology and many others. Whichever methodology you choose depends on your ontological and epistemological values, and the position you adopt as a researcher (see Chapters 2 and 3).

Data sources and evidence

Data and evidence are central pillars of all forms of research. You need to explain where you found your data, how you gathered them, how you interpreted and analysed them and generated evidence. Explaining all these things helps you show the methodological rigour of your research. You also need to emphasise the ethical care you demonstrated when fulfilling these aspects.

Findings and/or conclusions

Your findings and conclusions section is where you outline some of what you have found and make your provisional claim to knowledge. Always present your findings as provisional and communicate your understanding that you may be mistaken in your conclusions. Take care to say that you are aware of the need to test the validity of your conclusions against the critical evaluations of others.

Discussion

This is where you discuss the process and experience of doing the research, and whether you feel it has been successful or could have been done differently. You will also discuss the main ideas and findings, and consider whether they may be relevant for other people.

Significance

At this point, speak about the significance, or importance, of what you have done. Speak about your learning and how this may influence your continuing learning and potentially the learning of other people, as individuals, groups and organisations. Be clear about what doing the research has meant for you in terms of developing your professionalism and raising the profile of your profession in the public eye.

How Your Report Will Be Judged

Your report will be judged in terms of the expectations of the organisation you are writing it for. Workplaces have a specific set of expectations, as do higher education institutions. Here are some of the main ones (there are many others).

Reports are judged in terms of different sets of criteria. These include:

- technical matters such as accuracy of writing (dealt with above);

- content knowledge (what should go into an action research report) and form of text (how it is written);

- communicative capacity (quality of communication).

We focus on the last two here.

CONTENT AND FORM OF REPORTS – HOW ARE THEY JUDGED?

The expectations of workplace-based reports are more modest than those of academic reports. They include the following.

Judging the content and form of workplace-based reports

- Does the report show how learning influenced the improvement of practices? Can you show how studying your practice helped you to improve your prospecting, appointing, presenting and consolidating?

- Does the report take a narrative form? Action research reports are stories of real-life practices. They are often written in the first person: 'I did ...' or 'we did ...', not 'the researcher did ...'. You can write a story about how you studied your practice and transformed your learning into new insights. Story is used extensively in professional education development contexts (Clandinin 2013; Moon 2010). This area is wide open for development in a sales context. Salespeople tell fabulous stories of experience. Just imagine the rich resource if they were captured as scholarly accounts.

- Does the report show the completion of at least one action reflection cycle? Do you explain how you moved from initial question to some kind of provisional conclusion? This need not be a solution or answer, but you do need to come to a point where you think you have achieved something, even if it is to begin to improve your understanding. Some authors say you need to show a concrete outcome to your action enquiry – for example, that you have increased your number of prospects – but we do not share this view. We tend towards Dewey's (1963) stance, that improved learning is as important as improved behaviours.

- Does it explain how data were gathered and evidence generated? It is important not simply to tell a story of action, which could count as professional learning or action learning, but to explain how you gathered data and generated evidence, which are hallmarks of research.

- Does your report show that you conducted a collaborative enquiry, and explain who your research participants were?

- Does it show how you conducted the research ethically and paid attention to others' needs and wishes? Does it show how you negotiated your values and practices with colleagues and participants?

- Does the report show how your learning influenced the learning and actions of others in your company or organisation? Have you contributed to a learning culture? Have you managed to overcome obstructions? If so, how have you done this? If not, how will you manage to work with or around any obstacles to learning?

- Engagement with the literatures: you would be expected to engage with some of the content and research literatures of sales, but not necessarily with more philosophical matters.

Judging the content and form of academic reports

An academic report needs to show the above points, and others to do with demonstrating methodological rigour, capacity for critique and academic quality. They include the following:

- You state your claim to knowledge at the beginning of your text. You do this regardless of level of degree. At doctoral level your knowledge claim must be original.

- You explain your ontological positioning, especially in relation to customers and colleagues. This is especially important when you speak about wishing to improve relationships with customers and colleagues.

- Your text shows your capacity for critical reflection, that is, not to take anything for granted but to interrogate normative assumptions, both your own and other people's (see Habermas's criteria below). Expressing this kind of critique is essential in writing. This is where you consider whether what you have said has come from your own thinking or whether someone else taught you to think it. A good example is the idea of 'Orientalism' (Said 1995). 'Orientalism' is a term coined by non-oriental people, says Said, to suit their own colonising purposes. Similarly, when a salesperson complains about the need for more leads, is the lack of leads the real reason for their lack of success or perhaps a matter of their own capacity? Another way to speak about critique is to say that you problematise something. This does not mean it becomes a problem, more that you interrogate it and look for the hidden meanings and unquestioned assumptions.

- You engage critically with the literatures, that is, you read texts with a critical eye and select those you feel speak best to your situation, or that you disagree with. In scholarly writing you are expected to engage critically, develop arguments and defend your position.

- Theoretical and conceptual frameworks: these are the main concepts and themes you look for in the texts you read, and use to provide a scaffolding for your report. In this book we have used the conceptual frameworks of social relationships, collaborative enquiry, the new alienation and extended professionalism.

- Generative transformational processes are evident throughout the text. This refers to the idea that all things have the inherent capacity to self-organise and transform into better versions of themselves (see page 54). What appears to be an end point becomes a new beginning: a prospect transforms into a customer; presenting turns into a sale; the consolidation phase of a sale generates new needs and desires; an existing customer recommends friends as potential new customers. There is no end to anything. The secret of successful selling is to recognise that everything is renewable, including your own resources, and that, with intent and energy, you can transform a current situation into one that holds greater promise for more peaceful and productive work.

Winter (1989) wrote about judging the quality of action research reports. He said that a report needed to demonstrate six principles:

1. offer a reflective critique in which the author shows that they have reflected on their work and generated new research questions;

2. offer a dialectical critique which subjects all 'given' phenomena to critique, recognising their inherent tendency to change;

3. be a collaborative resource in which people act and learn as participants;

4. accept risk as an inevitable feature of creative practice;

5. demonstrate a plural structure which accommodates a multiplicity of viewpoints;

6.   show the transformational and harmonious relationship between theory and practice (Winter 1989: 43–65).

Judging your communicative capacity

This is a major area for consideration. It has to do with your capacity to communicate your messages so that your reader will see your meanings as clearly as possible. It emphasises the importance of knowing how to write and communicate effectively. Unless you do so, all your research and knowledge is in danger of not being heard because people will not be able to understand what you are saying. You simply have to learn and practise how to write for a reader.

Several theorists have produced criteria that you should use to judge the quality of your writing and the texts you produce. Here are two (see McNiff forthcoming, 2014 for further ideas).

Habermas (1976) says that when people are involved in speaking together (in your case, when you are speaking to others through your report), they need to aim for intersubjective understanding through the mutual sharing and consideration of ideas. Enabling people to do this requires a speech act or a text to show the following qualities:

- What is said or written is comprehensible. Does it make sense to the hearer/reader?

- It is truthful. Is the speaker/writer telling the truth? Can they be believed? Do they provide evidence to show this?

- It is authentic. For example, the researcher shows, over time and through interaction, that they have committed to living as fully as possible the values they espouse.

- It is appropriate to the context. The researcher shows how contextual (historical, cultural, social and other) matters need to be taken into consideration when trying to communicate something.

Barnett (1997) summarises these ideas as follows:

> *Any speech act can be interrogated in any one of four ways. Is it true? Does the account hang together? Do you really believe that? And is its*

> *form appropriate to the context? (Barnett 1997: 30, cited in Garrick 1998: 140).*

Foucault (2001) writes about *parrhesia* (Chapter 8), that is, the courage to speak one's truth, even in the face of the high risk of punishment. He said that when a speaker speaks the truth they demonstrate:

- frankness: the speaker believes what they say;

- truth: they know what truth is and can communicate it to others;

- courage: it takes courage to tell the truth;

- criticism: they are critical of what they or other people are saying – they do not take things at face value;

- duty: they recognise they have a responsibility to tell the truth.

The question for you when writing your report is whether you are prepared to demonstrate these qualities through your writing. Speaking the truth, especially in some business contexts, can be awfully risky, and you have to be prepared for the consequences if you do. This idea has particular relevance for the next section, which is about how you can use your writing to influence the creation of new futures for salespeople and your profession.

The Potential Influence of Your Writing

When you write you make yourself powerful. Writing is an intentionally political act: you make your voice heard in the world. When you write for a peer audience in sales you communicate that salespeople should be taken seriously as people who know what they are doing and can contribute to public debates about what counts as professionalism. When you write for a scholarly audience you become an activist in a field that sees itself as a gatekeeper of what counts as knowledge and who counts as a knower. Like Olsen and Worsham (2003) you highlight the distinction between being an academic and being an intellectual: traditionalist academics tend to comment on the status quo, without necessarily wishing to challenge or change it; intellectuals aim actively to change things. Butler (1999) for example speaks about the need to 'trouble discourses' by challenging what is taken for granted. Said (1994) speaks about the responsibility of intellectuals to challenge and not to let the status quo remain as it is, echoing Foucault's ideas about *parrhesia*. Writing becomes political activism.

Contemporary literatures and discourses about sales need challenging. We have outlined some of the reasons in this book, and at this point we wish to return to the issues voiced at the beginning, that is, the colonisation of the profession by those who position themselves as elites. It is difficult to ignore many aspects of this when they stare you in the face: for example, the delightful naivety of a published paper that speaks about the future of change agency while reserving capital letters for Sales Managers but not for lower case salespeople. There still seems to be an assumption in much of the business and sales literatures that salespeople are lower case functionaries dependent on close guidance from upper case Sales Managers. It is assumed that salespeople can acquire:

- product knowledge

- market knowledge

- customer knowledge

- self-knowledge

- role knowledge (Geiger 2011: 442)

but perhaps not produce practice-based knowledge, as the basis for generating theory.

In this book we are emphasising the need for salespeople to do this, that is, produce practice-based knowledge that can influence the development of new thinking and new practices for organisational change. Most importantly, it is this kind of knowledge that can close the theory-practice gap. In 2001, Keep and Ash outlined some conditions for doing so. They included the following:

> There needs to be more 'practitioner-type/evidence-based' literature compiled by practitioners, as they could now be seen and recognized as the new 'gurus' of 'change management'. The reality of organisational life, such as small organisations undertaking difficult issues, can be shown from a fully-rounded, 360° perspective by taking all sides of the fence into consideration (p. 300).

Sen (2007) also highlights the need to take a fully-rounded perspective. We need to resist the temptation to categorise ourselves in terms of one single classification, to identify ourselves as either managers or salespeople: to adopt an 'either-or' attitude. Perhaps we need to identify ourselves first and foremost as human beings, workers who share a life in a community who wish to do the best they can for their own and one another's wellbeing. This means learning together, acknowledging different strengths, capacities and responsibilities, and not trying to jockey for position power.

To achieve this situation, perhaps salespeople need to shape themselves into new identities, as activist change agents, perhaps even as coaches to sales managers, so all can learn how to share practices and break down divides. Keep and Ash comment on the role of change agents as having a responsibility to

> 'hold a mirror up' to the organisation, or to the client. This is part of the process of facilitation and change. ... While doing this, change agents may need help to hold a mirror up to themselves to reflect on their own practice – with the organization, or from an outsider, to gain balance, and grounding in what are sometimes difficult projects (2001: 299).

There are perhaps fewer more difficult yet more rewarding projects than to change one's self-perception but this is essential as a first step to changing one's image in the public domain. We authors have done this, so we know how difficult it can be. We both have a history of direct selling and continue with this work, while mixing it with consultancy work, writing and teaching. This is what we try to encourage you to do too. We hope that, through the book, we have encouraged you to see yourself as a competent and capable practitioner who is able to generate their own theory of practice and put it in the public domain so that others may learn with and from you. We hope we have influenced business and sales managers too. Sales is not only about selling string and sealing wax. It is about selling ideas and high aspirations. We hope the idea of researching your practice and generating your own theory of practice transforms into reality and that this book goes some way to helping you to do so.

Thank you for reading. Please connect through the email addresses at the front of the book and let us know how you get on. We cannot guarantee to have answers to any questions you may raise, but we can guarantee that you already have the means to create your own answers inside yourself. The excitement is in doing so.

References

Aldridge, A. (2003) *Consumption*. Cambridge, Blackwell.

Alford, C.F. (2001) *Whistleblowers: Broken Lives and Organizational Power*. Ithaca, NY, Cornell University Press.

Allport, G.W. (1961) *Pattern and Growth in Personality*. New York, Holt, Rinehart Winston.

Alvesson, M. (2013) *The Triumph of Emptiness: Consumption, Higher Education and Work Organization*. Oxford, Oxford University Press.

Appadurai, A. (1988) 'Introduction: Commodities and the politics of value' in Appadurai (ed.) *The Social Life of Things*. Cambridge, Cambridge University Press.

Apple, M. (2000) *Official Knowledge*. London, Routledge.

Archer, D. and Cameron, A. (2013) *Collaborative Leadership: Building Relationships, Handling Conflict and Sharing Control* (2nd edition). Abingdon, Routledge.

Arendt, H. (1958) *The Human Condition*. Chicago, University of Chicago Press.

Arendt, H. (1967) *Men in Dark Times*. New York, Harcourt, Brace & World.

Argyris, C. (1964) *Integrating the Individual and the Organization*. New York: Wiley.

Argyris, C. (1993) *Knowledge for Action. A Guide to Overcoming Barriers to Organizational Change*. San Francisco, Jossey Bass.

Argyris, C. and Schön, D. (1978) *Organizational Learning: A Theory of Action Perspective*. Reading, MA, Addison Wesley.

Argyris, C. and Schön, D. (1996) *Organizational Learning II: Theory, Method and Practice*. Reading, MA, Addison Wesley.

Armstrong, J.S. (2001) *Principles of Forecasting: A Handbook for Researchers and Practitioners*. Norwell, MA, Kluwer Academic Publishers.

Bachrach, B. (1996) *Values-Based Selling*. San Diego, CA, Aim High Publishing.

Bakhtin, M. (1981) *The Dialogic Imagination: Four Essays*. Austin, TX, University of Texas Press.

Ball, S. (2007) *Education plc*. Abingdon, Routledge.

Ball, S. (2012) *Global Education Inc*. Abingdon, Routledge.

Barnett, R. (1997) *Higher Education: A Critical Business*. Buckingham, The Society for Research into Higher Education and Open University Press.

Barnett, R. (2004) 'Learning for an unknown future', *Higher Education Research & Development* 23 (3): 247–260.

Baudrillard, J. (2005) *The System of Objects*. London, Verso.

Bauman, Z. (2005) *Work, Consumerism and the New Poor* (2nd edition). Maidenhead, Open University Press.

Berlin, I. (1990) (ed. H. Hardy) *The Crooked Timber of Humanity: Chapters in the History of Ideas*. London, Chatto & Windus.

Bohm, D. (ed. L. Nichols) (1996) *On Dialogue*. London, Routledge.

Bolton, G. (2010) *Reflective Practice* (3rd edition). London, Sage.

Bosworth, M. (1995) *Solution Selling*. New York, McGraw-Hill.

Bourdieu, P. (1990) *The Logic of Practice*. Cambridge, Polity.

Bourdieu, P. (1992) *Language and Symbolic Power* (ed. J.B. Thompson) (trans. G. Raymond and M. Adamson). London, Polity.

Branson, R. (2010) *Screw It, Let's Do It*. London, Virgin Books.

Brookfield, S. (1987) *Developing Critical Thinkers*. Buckingham, Open University Press.

Brookfield, S. (2013) *Powerful Techniques for Teaching in Lifelong Learning*. Maidenhead, Open University Press.

Brown, J.S. and Duguid, P. (2000) *The Social Life of Information*. Boston, MA, Harvard Business School Press.

Buber, M. (1937) *I and Thou*. (trans. R.G. Smith) Edinburgh, Clark.

Buehrer, R., Simon, L. and Bieraugel, M. (2013) 'Sales Research Sweet Spot: is academic research in sales and sales management relevant to practitioners? If it is relevant, is there a "sweet spot" between the academic research and the need for a more practitioner-friendly sales journal?' Paper presented at the National Conference in Sales Management, San Diego, April 3–6. Available online at http://www.ncsmweb.com/conference/2013-proceedings. Accessed 8 February 2014.

Butler, J. (1999) *Gender Trouble*. New York, Routledge.

Callahan, R. (1964) *Education and the Cult of Efficiency*. Chicago, University of Chicago Press.

Capra, F. (1996) *The Web of Life*. London, HarperCollins.

Carr, W. and Kemmis, S. (1986) *Becoming Critical: Education, Knowledge and Action Research*. London, The Falmer Press.

Carroll, D. (2012) *Managing Value in Organisations*. Abingdon, Gower.

Castells, M. (1996) *The Rise of the Network Society*. Malden, MA, Blackwell.

Cattell, R.B. (1965) *The Scientific Analysis of Personality*. Harmondsworth, Penguin.

Chomsky, N. (1986) *Knowledge of Language: Its Nature, Origin and Use*. New York, Praeger.

Chomsky, N. (2000) *Chomsky on MisEducation*. Lanham, Rowman & Littlefield.

Chomsky, N. (2001) *The Common Good*. Tucson, AZ, Odonian Press.

Chomsky, N. (2005) *Chomsky on Anarchism*. Oakland, CA, AK Press.

Chomsky, N. and Barsamian, D. (2001) *Propaganda and the Public Mind*. London, Pluto Press.

Clandinin, J. (2013) *Engaging in Narrative Inquiry (Developing Qualitative Inquiry)*. Walnut Creek, CA, Left Coast Press.

Cockerell, L. (2008) *Creating Magic*. London, Vermilion.

Cohen, L., Manion, L. and Morrison, K. (2011) *Research Methods in Education* (7th edition). Abingdon, Routledge.

Collingwood, R.G. (1939) *An Autobiography*. Oxford, Oxford University Press.

Collini, S. (2012) *What Are Universities For?* London, Penguin.

Cooper, M. (2009) *Who Really Runs Ireland?* Dublin, Penguin.

Cooper, M. (2011) *How Ireland Went Bust*. Dublin, Penguin.

Cooperrider, D.L., Whitney, D. and Stavros, J.M. (2008) *Appreciative Inquiry Handbook* (2nd edition) Brunswick, OH, Crown Custom Publishing.

Cranfield, J. (2007) *How to Get from Where You Are to Where You Want to Be*. London, HarperElement.

Crawshaw, S. and Jackson, J. (2010) *Small Acts of Resistance: How Courage, Tenacity and Ingenuity can Change the World*. New York, Union Square.

Creswell, J. (2007) *Qualitative Inquiry and Research Design* (2nd edition). Thousand Oaks, CA, Sage.

Csikszentmihalyi, M. (1990) *Flow: The Psychology of Optimal Experience*. New York, HarperPerennial.

Dadds, M. and Hart, S. (2001) *Doing Practitioner Research Differently*. Abingdon, Routledge.

Dawson, C. (2005) *Returning to Learning*. Oxford, How To Books.

Delves Broughton, P. (2009) *What They Teach You at Harvard Business School*. London, Penguin.

Delves Broughton, P. (2012) *The Art of the Sale*. New York, Penguin Press.

Dewey, J. (1916) *Democracy and Education*. New York, Free Press.

Dewey, J. (1963) *Experience and Education*. New York, Collier Books.

Drucker, P. (1967) *The Effective Executive*. New York, Harper and Row.

Dweck, C. (2012) *Mindset: How You Can Fulfil Your Potential*. London, Robinson.

Easterby-Smith, M., Burgoyne, J. and Araujo, L. (1999) *Organizational Learning and the Learning Organization*. London, Sage.

Eikeland, O. (2012) 'Action research – different conceptualisations, similar or different approaches?', *International Journal of Action Research* 8 (1): 5–9. Available online at http://www.academia.edu/1345823/Action_Research_Applied_Research_Intervention_Research_Collaborative_Research_Practitioner_Research_or_Praxis_Research. Accessed 25 October 2013.

Elkjaer, B. (2009) 'Pragmatism: a learning theory for the future', in K. Illeris (ed.) *Contemporary Theories of Learning*. Abingdon, Routledge.

Elliott, J. (1991) *Action Research for Educational Change*. Buckingham, Open University Press.

Elliott, J. (2007) *Reflecting Where the Action Is: The Selected Works of John Elliott.* Abdingon, Routledge.

Evans, L. (2008) 'Professionalism, professionality and the development of education professionals', *British Journal of Educational Studies* 56 (1): 20–38.

Eysenck, H.J. (1971) *Race, Intelligence and Education.* London, Temple-Smith.

Fals-Borda, O. (1982) 'Participatory research and rural social change', *Journal of Rural Cooperation* 10 (1): 25–39.

Fals Borda, O. and Rahman, M.A. (1991) *Action and Knowledge.* Lanham, MD, Rowman & Littlefield.

Fanghanel, J. (2012) *Being an Academic.* Abingdon, Routledge.

Feldman, A. (2003) 'Validity and quality in self-study', *Educational Researcher* 32 (3): 26–28.

Festinger, L. (1957) *A Theory of Cognitive Dissonance.* Stanford, CA, Stanford University Press.

Feynman, R. (1999) *The Meaning of It All.* London, Penguin.

Field, J. (2006) *Lifelong Learning and the New Educational Order* (2nd edition). Stoke-on-Trent, Trentham Books.

Flood, R. (1999) *Rethinking the Fifth Discipline.* London, Routledge.

Foucault, M. (1977) *Discipline and Punish.* Harmondsworth, Peregrine.

Foucault, M. (1980) (ed. C. Gordon) *Power/Knowledge: Selected Interviews and Other Writings: 1972–1977.* New York, Pantheon Books.

Foucault, M. (1997) 'The ethics of the concern for self as a practice of freedom', in P. Rabinow (ed.) *Michel Foucault: Ethics, Subjectivity and Truth: The Essential Works of Michel Foucault 1954–1984, Vol. 1.* Harmondsworth, Penguin.

Foucault, M. (2001) *Fearless Speech.* Los Angeles, CA, Semiotext(e).

Freire, P. (1993) (ed. P. McLaren and P. Leonard) *Paulo Freire: A Critical Encounter.* London, Routledge.

Freire, P. (1995) *Pedagogy of Hope. Reliving Pedagogy of the Oppressed.* New York, Continuum.

Freire, P. (1996) *Pedagogy of the Oppressed.* London, Penguin.

Fromm, E. (1956) *The Art of Loving.* New York, Harper & Row.

Fromm, E. (1979) *To Have or to Be.* New York, Abacus.

Garnett, J., Costley, C. and Workman, B. (eds) (2009) *Work Based Learning: Journeys to the Core of Higher Education.* Middlesex University, Middlesex University Press.

Garrick, J. (1998) *Informal Learning in the Workplace.* London, Routledge.

Garrison, D.R. (2011) *E-Learning in the 21st Century.* New York, Routledge.

Geiger, S. (2011) 'Salespeople's self-management: knowledge, emotions and behaviours', in P. Guenzi and S. Geiger (eds) *Sales Management: A Multinational Perspective.* London, Palgrave Macmillan.

Gibbons, M., Limoges, C., Nowotny, H., Schwartzman, S., Scott, P. and Trow, M. (1994) *The New Production of Knowledge: The Dynamics of Science and Research in Contemporary Societies*. London, Sage.

Gilfoyle, T. (1994) *City of Eros: New York, Prostitution and the Commercialisation of Sex, 1790–1920*. New York, W.W. Norton & Company.

Girard, J. (1989) *How to Close Every Sale*. New York, Warner Books.

Ghaye, T. (2011) *Teaching and Learning through Reflective Practice*. Abingdon, Routledge.

Goodson, I. (2013) *Developing Narrative Theory*. Abingdon, Routledge.

Green, C. (2006) *Trust-Based Selling*. New York, McGraw-Hill.

Greenwood, D. And Levin, M. (2007) *Introduction To Action Research* (2nd Edition). Thousand Oaks, CA, Sage.

Guenzi, P. and Geiger, S. (eds) (2011) *Sales Management: A Multinational Perspective*. Basingsoke, Palgrave Macmillan.

Habermas, J. (1972) *Knowledge and Human Interests* (trans. J.J. Shapiro). London, Heinemann.

Habermas, J. (1975) *Legitimation Crisis*. Boston, MA, Beacon Press.

Habermas, J. (1976) *Communication and the Evolution of Society*. Boston, MA, Beacon.

Habermas, J. (1987) *The Theory of Communicative Action: Volume 2: The Critique of Functionalist Reason*. Oxford, Polity.

Handy, E. and Handy, C. (2002) *Reinvented Lives: Women at Sixty: A Celebration*. London, Hutchinson.

Hannerz, U. (1990) 'Cosmopolitans and locals in world culture', *Theory, Culture & Society* 7, 237–251. Available online at http://tcs.sagepub.com. Accessed 16 June, 2013.

Hargreaves, A. (2003) *Teaching in the Knowledge Society: Education in the Age of Insecurity*. New York, Teachers College Press.

Harland, T. and Pickering, N. (2011) *Values in Higher Education Teaching*. Abingdon, Routledge.

Hawken, P. (2010) (Revised edition) *The Ecology of Commerce*. New York, HarperCollins.

Henderson, H. (1996) *Building a Win-Win World*. San Francisco, CA, Berrett-Koehler.

Hermans, H. and Gieser, T. (eds) (2012) *Handbook of Dialogical Self Theory*. Cambridge, NY, Cambridge University Press.

Herr, K. and Anderson, G. (2005) *The Action Research Dissertation: A Guide for Students and Faculty*. Thousand Oaks, CA, Sage.

Hoe, S. and Roebuck, D. (1999) *The Taking of Hong Kong: Charles and Clara Elliot in China Waters*. Richmond, The Curzon Press.

Hopkins, T. (1982) *How to Master the Art of Selling*. New York, Warner Books.

Hoyle, E. (1975) 'Professionality, professionalism and control in teaching', in V. Houghton et al. (eds) *Management in Education: the Management of Organisations and Individuals*. London, Ward Lock Educational.

Inglis, T. (2008) *Global Ireland: Same Difference*. London, Routledge.

James, O. (2007) *Affluenza*. London, Vermilion.

Jenkins, M. (1997) *The Customer-Centred Strategy*. London, Pitman.

Johnson, A. (2002) *A Short Guide to Action Research*. Boston, MA, Allyn and Bacon.

Johnson, S. (2001) *Emergence: The Connected Lives of Ants, Brains, Cities and Software*. London, Allen Lane, The Penguin Press.

Johnston, M. and Marshall, G. (2013) *Contemporary Selling*. New York, Routledge.

Jolles, R. (2000) *Customer Centered Selling*. New York, Simon & Schuster.

Kahneman, D. (2011) *Thinking, Fast and Slow*. London, Penguin.

Kahneman, D. and Tversky, A. (eds) (2000) *Choices, Values and Frames*. New York, Cambridge University Press.

Kahneman, D., Knatch, J. and Thaler, R. (1990) 'Experimental test of the endowment effect and the Coase Theorem', *Journal of Political Economy* 98 (6): 1325–1348.

Kauffman, S. (1995) *At Home in the Universe: The Search for Laws of Self-Organization and Complexity*. London, Viking.

Keep, J. and Ash, K. (2001) 'Change agency practice – the future', in B. Hamlin, J. Keep and K. Ash (eds) *Organizational Change and Development*. Harlow, Pearson Education.

Kemmis, S. (1982) 'Action research', in T. Husen and T. Postlethwaite (eds) *International Encyclopaedia of Education: Research & Studies*. Oxford, Pergamon Press.

Kemmis, S. (2009) 'Action research as a practice-based practice', *Educational Action Research* 17 (3): 463–474.

Kemmis, S. and Heikkinen, H.L.T. (2012) 'Practice architectures and teacher induction', in H.L.T. Heikkinen, H. Jokinen and P. Tynjälä (eds) *Peer-group Mentoring (PGM): Peer Group Mentoring for Teachers' Professional Development*. London, Routledge.

Kim E. and Yoon D.J. (2012) 'Why does service with a smile make employees happy? A social interaction model', *The Journal of Applied Psychology* 97 (6): 1059–1067.

Kirwan, C. (2013) *Making Sense of Organizational Learning*. Farnham, Gower.

Klein, N. (2000) *No Logo*. New York, Picador.

Kolb, D. A. (1984) *Experiential Learning. Experience as the Source of Learning and Development*. Englewood Cliffs, NJ: Prentice Hall.

Krog, A. (2003) *A Change of Tongue*. Johannesburg, Random House.

Kuhn, T. (1996) *The Structure of Scientific Revolutions* (3rd Edition). London, University of Chicago Press.

Kushner, S. (2000) *Personalizing Evaluation*. London, Sage.

Langer, E. (2010) *Counterclockwise*. London, Hodder.

Lankshear, C. and Knobel, M. (2011) *Literacies: Social, Cultural and Historical Perspectives*. New York, Peter Lang.

Lave, J. and Wenger, E. (1991) *Situated Learning: Legitimate Peripheral Participation*. Cambridge, Cambridge University Press.

Law, J. (2004) *After Method: Mess in Social Science Research*. London, Routledge.

Lee, N. and Kotler, P. (2011) *Social Marketing: Influencing Behaviors for Good*. New York, Sage.

Lewin, K. (1946) 'Action research and minority problems', *Journal of Social Issues*, 2 (4): 34–46.

Lilla, M. (2001) *The Reckless Mind: Intellectuals in Politics*. New York, New York Review of Books.

Littlechild, B. and Smith, R. (2013) *A Handbook for Interprofessional Practice in the Human Services*. Harlow, Pearson.

Lyotard, J.-F. (1984) *The Postmodern Condition: A Report on Knowledge*. Manchester, Manchester University Press.

Macdonald, B.J. (1995) (ed.) *Theory as a Prayerful Act: The Collected Essays of James B. Macdonald*. New York, Peter Lang.

Macfarlane, B. (2007) *The Academic Citizen: The Virtue of Service in University Life*. Abingdon, Routledge.

Macmurray, J. (1957) *The Self as Agent*. London, Faber and Faber.

Macmurray, J. (1961) *Persons in Relation*. London, Faber and Faber.

Marcuse, H. (1964) *One-Dimensional Man*. Boston, MA, Beacon.

Marr, A. (2012) *A History of the World*. London, Pan.

Martin, R. (2011) *Fixing the Game: How Runaway Expectations Broke the Economy and How to Get Back to Reality*. Boston, MA, Harvard Business Review Press.

Marx, K. (2013) *The Eighteenth Brumaire of Louis Bonaparte*. (E-Book, online at http://www.gutenberg.org/files/1346/1346-h/1346-h.htm.) Accessed 25 October 2013.

Maslow, A. (1954) *Motivation and Personality*. New York, Harper & Row.

Maslow, A. (1968) *Towards a Psychology of Being*. New York, Wiley.

Mason, J. (2010) *Qualitative Researching*. Thousand Oaks, CA, Sage.

McDonnell, P. and McNiff, J. (in preparation) *Action Research for Nursing* (working title).

McNay, I. (1995) 'From collegial academy to the corporate enterprise: the changing cultures of universities', in T. Schuller (ed.) *The Changing University*. Maidenhead, The Open University.

McNiff, J. (1984) 'Action research: a generative model for in-service support', *British Journal of In-Service Education*, 10 (3): 40–46.

McNiff, J. (1989) *An Explanation for an Individual's Educational Development through the Dialectic of Action Research*. PhD thesis, University of Bath.

McNiff, J. (2002) *Action Research: Principles and Practice* (2nd edition). London, Routledge.

McNiff, J. (2010) *Action Research for Professional Development: Concise Advice for New and Experienced Action Researchers*. Poole, September.

McNiff, J. (2013a) *Action Research: Principles and Practice* (3rd edition). Abingdon, Routledge.

McNiff, J. (2013b) 'Becoming cosmopolitan and other dilemmas of internationalisation', *Cambridge Journal of Education* 43 (4): 501–515.

McNiff, J. (forthcoming, 2014) *Writing and Doing Action Research*. London, Sage.

McNiff, J. and Whitehead, J. (2010) *You and Your Action Research Project* (3rd edition). Abingdon, Routledge.

McNiff, J. and Whitehead, J. (2011) *All You Need to Know about Action Research* (2nd edition). London, Sage.

Mellor, N. (1998) 'Notes from a method', *Educational Action Research* 6 (3): 453–470.

Mezirow, J. (2009) 'An overview on transformative learning', in K. Illeris (ed.) *Contemporary Learning Theories*. Abingdon, Routledge.

Mezirow, J. and Associates (2000) *Learning as Transformation*. San Francisco, CA, Jossey-Bass.

Miller, A. (1994) *Death of a Salesman*. London, Pearson Education.

Miller, R. (2002) *Free Schools, Free People: Education and Democracy after the 1960s*. Albany, NY, State University of New York Press.

Miller, R.B. and Heiman, S.E. (1998) *The New Strategic Selling*. New York, Business Plus.

Mitroff, I. and Linstone, H. (1995) *The Unbounded Mind: Breaking the Chains of Traditional Business Thinking*. Oxford, Oxford University Press.

Molenaar, C. (2013) *The End of Shops: Social Buying and the Battle for the Consumer*. Abingdon, Gower.

Moon, J. (2010) *Using Story*. Abingdon, Routledge.

Moran, J.W. and Brightman, B.K. (2001) 'Leading organizational change', *Career Development International* 6 (2/3): 111–121.

Morgan, G. (2006) *Images of Organization* (3rd edition). Thousand Oaks, CA, Sage.

Mullins, L. (2013) *Management and Organisational Behaviour* (3rd edition). Harlow, Pearson.

Noffke, S. (1997) 'Themes and tensions in US action research: towards historical analysis', in S. Hollingsworth (ed.), *International Action Research: A Casebook for Educational Reform*. London, Falmer.

Nonaka, I. and Takeuchi, H. (1995) *The Knowledge-Creating Company*. Oxford, Oxford University Press.

Nussbaum, M. (1997) *Cultivating Humanity*. Cambridge, MA, Harvard University Press.

Olssen, M. and Peters, M. (2005) 'Neoliberalism, higher education and the knowledge economy: from the free market to knowledge capitalism', *Journal of Educational Policy*, 30 (3): 313–345.

Olson, G. and Worsham, L. (eds) (2003) *Critical Intellectuals on Writing*. Albany, NY, State University of New York Press.

Open University (2005) *Action Research: A Guide for Associate Lecturers*. Available online at http://www.open.ac.uk/cobe/docs/AR-Guide-final.pdf. Accessed 25 October 2013.

O'Toole, F. (2009) *Ship of Fools*. London, Faber and Faber.

Packard, V. (1967) *The Hidden Persuaders*. London, Pelican.

Packer, G. (2007) *The Assassins' Gate: America in Iraq*. London, Faber and Faber.

Parkin, P. (2010) *Managing Change in Healthcare Using Action Research*. London, Sage.

Pearson, J. (2011) 'Adapting the boundaries in primary physical education: an account of my learning, my educational influence and improved practice', *Educational Action Research* 19 (4): 503–515.

Pink, D. (2012) *To Sell Is Human*. New York, Riverhead Books.

Polanyi, M. (1958) *Personal Knowledge*. London, Routledge & Kegan Paul.

Polanyi, M. (1967) *The Tacit Dimension*. New York, Doubleday.

Popper, K (2002) *The Poverty of Historicism*. London, Routledge.

Pressfield, S. (2011) *Do the Work! Overcome Resistance and Get Out of Your Own Way*. The Domino Project, powered by Amazon.com

Putnam, R.D. (2000) *Bowling Alone*. New York, Simon & Schuster

Rand, A. (1964) *The Virtue of Selfishness*. London, Signet.

Reason, P. and Bradbury, H. (eds) (2008) *The SAGE Handbook of Action Research* (2nd edition). London, Sage.

Ritzer, G. (2008) *The McDonaldization of Society 5*. Thousand Oaks, Pine Forge Press.

Robinson, K. (2011) *Out of Our Minds: Learning to be Creative* (updated edition). Chichester, Wiley.

Robson, C. (2011) *Real World Research* (3rd edition). Chichester, Wiley.

Rolfe, G. (1996) *Closing the Theory-Practice Gap: A New Paradigm for Nursing*. Oxford, Butterworth-Heinemann.

Rolfe, G. (1998) *Expanding Nursing Knowledge*. Oxford, Butterworth-Heinemann.

Ross, S. (2009) *The Bankers*. Dublin, Penguin.

Sachs, J. (2003) *The Activist Teaching Profession*. Buckingham, Open University Press.

Said, E (1994) *Representations of the Intellectual*. The 1993 Reith Lectures. London, Vintage.

Said, E. (1995) *Orientalism*. London, Penguin.

Said, E. (1997) *Beginnings: Intention and Method*. London, Granta.

Sajtos, L. (2011) 'Formulation of the sales programme: defining sales force investment and structure', in P. Guenzi and S. Geiger (eds) *Sales Management: A Multinational Perspective*. Basingstoke, Palgrave Macmillan.

Schmitt, B. (2003) *Customer Experience Management*. Hoboken, NJ, John Wiley & Sons.

Schön, D. (1973) *Beyond the Stable State*. New York, W.W. Norton & Company.

Schön, D. (1983) *The Reflective Practitioner*. New York, Basic Books.

Schön, D. (1995) 'Knowing-in-action: the new scholarship requires a new epistemology', *Change*, November–December: 27–34.

Schön, D. and Rein, M. (1994) *Frame Reflection*. New York, Basic Books.

Schrage, M. (1990) *Down With Teams! Mastering the Dynamics of Creative Collaboration*. New York, Currency.

Schroeder, A. (2009) *The Snowball: Warren Buffett and the Business of Life*. New York, Bantam Books.

Schuller, T. and Watson, D. (2009) *Learning through Life: Inquiry into the Future of Lifelong Learning: Summary*. Leicester, National Institute of Adult Continuing Education (NIACE). Available online at http://www.niace.org.uk/lifelonglearninginquiry/docs/IFLL-summary-english.pdf. Accessed 25 October 2013.

Seligman, M. (2011) *Flourish*. London, Nicholas Brealey.

Sen, A. (2007) *Identity and Violence*. London, Penguin.

Senge, P. (1990) *The Fifth Discipline*. New York, Doubleday.

Senge, P., Scharmer, O., Jaworski, J. and Flowers, B.S. (2005) *Presence: Exploring Profound Change in People, Organizations and Society*. London, Nicholas Brealey.

Sennett, R. (1998) *The Corrosion of Character*. New York, W.W. Norton & Company.

Sennett, R. (2008) *The Craftsman*. London, Penguin.

Soros, G. (1998) *The Crisis of Global Capitalism*. London, Little, Brown and Company.

Spinoza, B. de (1996) (trans. E. Curley) *Ethics*. London, Penguin.

Stenhouse, L. (1975) *An Introduction to Curriculum Research and Development*. London, Heinemann.

Stringer, E. (2007) *Action Research* (3rd edition). Thousand Oaks, CA, Sage.

Swartz, D. (1997) *Culture and Power: The Sociology of Pierre Bourdieu*. Chicaco, University of Chicago Press.

Teixeira, P. and Dill, D. (eds) (2011) *Public Vices, Private Virtues?* Rotterdam, Sense Publishers.

Theroux, P. (1986) *Sunrise with Seamonsters*. Harmondsworth, Penguin.

Torbert, W.R. (2001) *The Power of Balance*. Newbury Park, CA, Sage.

Torbert, W.R. (2008) 'The practice of action inquiry', in P. Reason and H. Bradbury (eds) *Handbook of Action Research: Participative Inquiry and Practice*. London, Sage.

Tovey, D. (2012) *Principled Selling*. London, Kogan Page.

Tracy, B. (1996) *Advanced Selling Strategies*. New York, Simon and Schuster.

Tsang, A.K.T. (2013) *The Strategies and Skills Learning Development System*. Toronto, University of Toronto Press.

UNESCO (2013) *UNESCO Future Forum: Exploring the Dynamics of Knowledge Societies: Using the Future to Shape Transformative Policies*. Available online at http://www.unesco.org/new/en/bureau-of-strategic-planning/themes/anticipation-and-foresight/unesco-future-forums/exploring-the-dynamics-of-knowledge-societies/. Accessed 8 February 2014.

Varga, S. (2009) *Brilliant Pitch*. Harlow, Pearson Education.

Vlăsceanu, L. (2010) *Universities and Reflexive Modernity*. Budapest, Central University Press.

Watkinson, M. (2013) *The Ten Principles Behind Great Customer Experiences*. Harlow, Pearson.

Wenger, E. (1999) *Communities of Practice*. Cambridge, Cambridge University Press.

Wheatley, M. (1992) *Leadership and the New Science: Learning about Organization from an Orderly Universe*. San Francisco, CA., Berrett-Koehler.

Willcock, D. (2013) *Collaborating for Results*. Abingdon, Gower.

Winter, R. (1989) *Learning from Experience*. London, Falmer.

Winter, R. (1998) 'Managers, spectators and citizens: where does "theory" come from in action research?', *Educational Action Research* 6 (3): 361–376.

Witkin, R. (2003) *Adorno on Popular Culture*. London, Routledge.

Yin, R. (2009) *Case Study Research: Design and Methods* (4th edition). Thousand Oaks, CA, Sage.

Zikmund, W. (2003) *Business Research Methods* (7th edition). Mason, OH, Thomson South Western.

Zinn, H. (2005) *People's History of the United States*. New York, Harper Perennial.

Zuber-Skerritt, O. (1993) 'Improving Learning and Teaching Through Action Learning and Action Research', *Higher Education Research and Development* 12 (1): 45–58.

Index